MW00941604

YOU ARE NOT ALONE

Seeing Your Struggles
Through the Eyes of God

SHIRLEY PERICH

ZONDERVAN®

ZONDERVAN.com/
AUTHORTRACKER
follow your favorite authors

invert

youth
specialties

**youth
specialties**

You Are Not Alone

Copyright 2009 by Shirley Perich

Youth Specialties products, 300 S. Pierce St., El Cajon, CA 92020 are published by

Zondervan, 5300 Patterson Ave. SE, Grand Rapids, MI 49530.

Library of Congress Cataloging-in-Publication Data

Perich, Shirley.

    You are not alone : seeing your struggles through the eyes of God /

    Shirley Perich.

        p. cm.

    ISBN 978-0-310-28532-8

      1. Christian teenagers—Religious life. 2. Self-esteem in

    adolescence—Religious aspects—Christianity. 3. Identity

    (Psychology)—Religious aspects—Christianity. I. Title.

    BVV4531.3.P465 2008

    248.8'3 — dc22

                                               2008028016

Cover & interior design by David Conn

Printed in the United States of America

09 10 11 12 • 20 19 18 17 16 15 14 13 12 11 10 9 8 7 6 5 4 3 2 1

TABLE OF CONTENTS

FOR JUSTIN AND EVAN.

PREFACE

Nobody knows how I feel. Nobody knows what it's like to be me.

We've all been there.

And when you're there, you feel alone.

But you're not.

Every emotion you've ever experienced has been felt by all of humanity at one time or another.

Still feel alone?

You're not.

There is a God.

And he's not on vacation.

"Never will I leave you; never will I forsake you." (Hebrews 13:5) Can we trust God on that?

Don't toss this book into the garage sale pile until you know the answer.

CHAPTER 1

SOMETIMES I FEEL SMALL

A lot of people thought Jesus was a crazy homeless guy. The world was looking for a savior, a king, a warrior, a guy in a palace. He wasn't what they expected, so a lot of people missed him. But once you get to know him, you realize pulling off the unexpected is a recurring theme with Jesus.

Who would've guessed the architect of the universe wouldn't even put a roof over his own head?

Or the Source of all knowledge and wisdom would appear to have lost his marbles because of the wild things he said? Even his family wondered about him.

And wait 'til you hear about the crowd Jesus ran around with.

You have Matthew, the tax collector, who, on a pretty sure bet, was lining his pockets with poor people's hard-earned denari.

Peter, James, and John were average guys who caught fish for a living.

Mary Magdalene may or may not have been a prostitute, but we know at the very least she had some issues. Coexisting with several demons doesn't land you on the short list of many gala events.

Jesus had dinner with men who cheated people, and he forgave women who cheated on their husbands. He worked, walked, and talked with people just like you and me.

We'd expect to find him among the powerful and popular of Galilee. But Jesus wasn't looking for people who didn't think they needed him. He was looking for people the world had overlooked. When he found them—

He loved 'em.

He changed 'em.

And he used 'em

(You, too, but we'll talk about that later.)

Jesus didn't see their social status. He didn't hold their poor decisions against them. He saw their hearts. That meant he saw their pain. And he loved them.

(You, too, but we'll talk about that later.)

He healed them.

He encouraged them.

He brought out the best in them.

He challenged them.

He championed them.

He hung out with them.

He honored them.

He prayed for them.

He blessed them.

He was their friend.

Jesus was one of those love-you-at-all-costs-through-thick-and-thin-whether-you're-messy-or-even-messier kinds of friends.

(Yours, too, but we'll talk about that later—so don't lose this book.)

I'LL CALL NOBODIES AND MAKE THEM SOMEBODIES; I'LL CALL THE UNLOVED AND MAKE THEM BELOVED. (ROMANS 9:25 MSG)

(Now that ain't small potatoes.)

And remember those ordinary fishermen? They didn't stay ordinary for long.

Friends of Jesus rarely do.

BUT SEEING THE BOLDNESS OF PETER AND JOHN, AND PERCEIVING THAT THEY WERE UNLETTERED AND UNINSTRUCTED MEN, THEY WONDERED; AND THEY RECOGNISED THEM THAT THEY WERE WITH JESUS. (ACTS 4:13 DARBY)

Make 'em wonder.

CHAPTER 2

SOMETIMES I FEEL GUILTY

If a simple squirt, squeeze, or pump of a bottle can produce hair that's volumized, curled, straightened, conditioned, shined, styled, and managed—we're there. White teeth? Smooth skin? We're all over it.

We care about how we look. There's a mega-billion-dollar beauty industry that tells us so.

And scents? There's no excuse to smell bad in this day and age. We'll even hang cardboard pineapples in our cars just in case our noses might come in contact with anything less than pineappley.

That's okay. In fact, it's good. You should want to be, look, and smell your best. Do it for your family, your friends, and the door greeter at Wal-Mart. But don't do it for God...even if you could benefit from a cardboard pineapple around your neck.

See, you may not smell so good.

You may get high.

You may get drunk and act stupid.

You may have lost your virginity.

You may have had an abortion.

You may be disrespectful.

You may cheat.

You may steal stuff.

You may lie.

You may be lazy.

And while you may not want the world to know what's going on behind the deodorant, don't worry about God.

Go to God just the way you are and say, "Lord, here I am. Sorry about the garbage I've brought with me. It's kind of heavy, and the smell isn't even close to the pineapple family. Mind if I set it right here at your feet?"

He'll say, "Sure, give it all to me. I've been waiting to take it—that may sound a little crazy, but I paid a hefty price just so I could claim all this as my own."

While you wouldn't expect the world to want to see, smell, look at, or deal with your garbage, Jesus is actually waiting for it.

Doesn't that blow you away just a little bit?

HE RAISES THE POOR FROM THE DUST AND LIFTS THE NEEDY FROM THE ASH HEAP. (PSALM 113:7)

You may feel that *poor* and *needy* don't apply to you. But those conditions don't only refer to your bank account or wallet. They also refer to the condition of your heart. And until you've unloaded the garbage, poor and needy is where we all are.

Jesus wants all your wrongs, hurts, and sorrows because he paid for them with his life. He loves you just that much.

But understand something: If you don't love him back, if you choose your way instead of his, then you keep your garbage. But this love of his still stands. It's a done deal. And it doesn't shrink with every mistake, either. It is always there.

See, Jesus doesn't love you because of who you are—even if you are pretty adorable. Jesus loves you because of who *he* is.

His love is big.

His love never ends.

His love is unconditional.

Now I call that some good news. Quite frankly, I've danced around the room and hugged my mom for less.

HE WILL TAKE GREAT DELIGHT IN YOU; IN HIS LOVE HE WILL NO LONGER REBUKE YOU, BUT WILL REJOICE OVER YOU WITH SINGING. (ZEPHANIAH 3:17)

CHAPTER 3

SOMETIMES I FEEL UNFORGIVABLE

All that garbage we just got rid of? God hates it.

And while Jesus readily takes it, don't think it doesn't have to be reconciled, forgiven, or atoned for. Feeling better? Probably not. That's why we're spending one more chapter on it.

Here's the good news: The reconciling, forgiving, and atoning isn't your job.

Jesus did that. He died an ugly death on an ugly cross in order to pay the price for all the ugliness in the world.

Ever wonder what big landfill all this garbage ends up in? Somehow I have a feeling God anticipated our question, because the answer we find in the Bible doesn't lack clarity or power.

YOU WILL TREAD OUR SINS UNDERFOOT AND HURL ALL OUR INIQUITIES INTO THE DEPTHS OF THE SEA. (MICAH 7:19)

That might not be far enough for you, so how about this?

AS FAR AS THE EAST IS FROM THE WEST, SO FAR HAS HE REMOVED OUR TRANSGRESSIONS FROM US. (PSALM 103:12)

Once you've asked for forgiveness, God doesn't remember your sins. But just between you and me, Satan would love to have you continue to beat yourself up over all the embarrassing and shameful things you've said, done, and thought.

Really, that makes his day. In fact, he'll go to great lengths to torment you with your past. Yes, torment. Don't open the door for him— even a crack. He never brings a party with him.

But Satan does something more. He makes God out to be a liar. If you'll remember back to the Garden of Eden, you'll know that this is one of Satan's specialties (Genesis 3). He likes to make you doubt the finality of God's forgiveness. Satan really trips up a lot of people with this, so let's not go any farther without putting this to rest.

Satan is famous for saying, "Yeah, God says you're forgiven, but remember what you've done? Why would God wipe *that* away? No, my fellow loser-friend, you can be quite sure you'll have to carry around that hideous past of yours for quite some time. Maybe forever."

He may even have you thinking, *Good point. I can't forget it, so why should I expect God to?*

Well, you can expect God to forget it because he said he would.

I, EVEN I, AM HE WHO BLOTS OUT YOUR TRANSGRESSIONS, FOR MY OWN SAKE, AND REMEMBERS YOUR SINS NO MORE. (ISAIAH 43:25)

God keeps promises.

You're forgiven.

You're his.

And you can take that to the bank.

Now we've come to the part where you smile.

C'mon. A big one.

(Make everybody wonder what you're reading.)

CHAPTER 4

SOMETIMES I FEEL WORRIED

Know what makes a lot of us sweat? And worry?

Details.

Why? Because details often trip us up and cause us to fail.

They're just so unpredictable. A lot of them are unwelcome. Some we handily dismiss but others move in with their bags and require us to entertain them for way too long. Top that off with our inability to anticipate or avoid their arrival, and you know what we are?

On edge.

And most likely sweating.

But know what God loves to handle?

You got it. Details.

IT CAME AS A SHEER GIFT TO ME, A REAL SURPRISE, GOD HANDLING ALL THE DETAILS...GOD SAW TO IT THAT I WAS EQUIPPED, BUT YOU CAN BE SURE THAT IT HAD NOTHING TO DO WITH MY NATURAL ABILITIES. (EPHESIANS 3:7-8 MSG)

It's amazing. God gives us what we need (strength, wisdom, courage, etc.) to face situations beyond our natural abilities. Understanding this concept puts worry in its place. Once you have a handle on it you can sell this advice to everyone you know.

Just kidding. Don't sell it.

So here's a little equipping beyond natural ability for you. A long time ago in the land of Egypt the children of Israel lived as slaves for many years. (If you feel a story coming on, you're right, so get comfortable. Pause the book. Grab a snack. Get a drink. We'll wait. Ready?)

Okay. We're in the book of Exodus and we find God's people living as slaves. They were required to work hard, long days for the Pharaoh of Egypt. Finally their day of deliverance from this life of servitude came. The Lord gave them a leader named Moses and the green light to pack their things. They were on their way to a place prepared especially for them. Ahhh...free at last.

Wouldn't you know, a funny thing happened on the way to the Promised Land. Certainly they weren't able to take care of details with a quick check of Mapquest for the best route out of town. They had the entire Egyptian army tailing them because, when it came right down to it, Pharaoh really didn't want his labor force leaving. Who was going to make the bricks? Good free help is hard to find, and Pharaoh knew it.

So, we have a Red Sea without a bridge; horses, chariots, and warriors coming up from behind; no game plan. Minor details.

Perhaps a little concern is understandable. About now Moses was hearing two million people crabbin' at him. It doesn't take long for the grumbling to start. When you're in a pickle, it's easy to grumble. And worry.

This is more than a story about people living a long time ago in a far-away land, but I think you knew that. We all have Red Seas in our lives that get in our way, ruin our days, and make us grumble. And worry.

We have a situation here that really should've been the last chapter in the Old Testament—but instead becomes one of the Lord's mightiest hours.

Ever have one of those *last chapter* kinds of days? Ever feel certain unsuspecting divers will discover your body at the bottom of the Red Sea?

Here's where God's *equipping beyond natural abilities* comes in—and not a minute too soon. The Lord told Moses to raise his shepherd's staff and hold his hand over the sea to divide the water. Parting bodies of water wasn't a natural ability Moses possessed. But Moses obeyed, God's children crossed safely, and the bad guys drowned. Who among the Israelites envisioned *that* as they packed their bags that morning? God sure isn't short on surprises.

And he doesn't change!

He went before them.

He'll go before you.

I WILL GO BEFORE YOU AND WILL LEVEL THE MOUNTAINS; I WILL BREAK DOWN GATES OF BRONZE AND CUT THROUGH BARS OF IRON. (ISAIAH 45:2)

With a God like that you can sleep a little sounder and walk a little taller. You carry a stick as big as Moses did.

YOU HEM ME IN BEHIND AND BEFORE, AND YOU LAY YOUR HAND UPON ME. (PSALM 139:5)

So, what are you worried about? Worry sets in when we forget just how good and mighty our God is.

You never know exactly how God's going to take care of those details.

God has paths for you to walk down you don't even know exist. This is one crazy adventure, my friend.

YOUR ROAD LED THROUGH THE SEA, YOUR PATHWAY THROUGH THE MIGHTY WATERS—A PATHWAY NO ONE KNEW WAS THERE! (PSALM 77:19 NLT)

Never make God small.

He's way bigger than anything you can find to worry about.

CHAPTER 5

SOMETIMES I FEEL APPREHENSIVE

Despite the Israelites' miraculous send-off from Egypt (see Chapter 4), the next phase of their trip toward the Promised Land made God's people unsure about their future. Unknowns can throw the best of us into a tailspin. Unknowns make us feel apprehensive.

Trusting in one's own resources can do that, too. The next scene in the Israelites' journey is just such a case study. (Check it out in Deuteronomy.) Misplaced reliance on their own strength sent them back out to the desert for the next 40 years.

They died out there. Their children didn't, but they did. And it didn't have to be that way.

In hopes of keeping our own apprehensive selves out of self-made deserts for years on end, it's in our best interest to understand and learn from the Israelites' mistakes. So, here's a little more of their story based on Numbers 13.

When they got near the Promised Land, they sent 12 spies to go in and check out the situation. What they saw was indeed, just as promised, a beautiful land. A land with big fruit and big people. The big fruit didn't freak them out, but the big people did.

They felt like grasshoppers next to these giants (their words, not mine).

But Moses said:

> "DO NOT BE TERRIFIED; DO NOT BE AFRAID OF THEM. THE LORD YOUR GOD, WHO IS GOING BEFORE YOU, WILL FIGHT FOR YOU AS HE DID FOR YOU IN EGYPT, BEFORE YOUR VERY EYES." (DEUTERONOMY 1:29-30)

Understand how powerful those words are. Understand them because they're being spoken to YOU. That battle was not to be won through their own strength.

None of yours are, either.

Do you think they would've lost to these giants? Do you think you'll lose to the giants in your life?

Even though the Israelites had seen the Lord provide for them in so many cool and outrageous ways, they couldn't quite trust him with this *giant-people* thing. (Need I mention all the giant-fill-in-the-blank things in our lives we don't trust God with?)

Now does it seem logical that God would carry the Israelites over the barren, treacherous desert and then dump them in the lap of some giants to be eaten alive? I ask you.

See, they forgot something. We do, too. Often. So Moses reminded them—and us:

"THERE [IN THE WILDERNESS] YOU SAW HOW THE Lord YOUR GOD CARRIED YOU, AS A FATHER CARRIES HIS SON, ALL THE WAY YOU WENT UNTIL YOU REACHED THIS PLACE." (DEUTERONOMY 1:31)

There's no lack of tenderness in this imagery, is there? A little reminder about how precious we are to God does one's heart good.

Okay, one more for good measure since we so easily forget:

LIKE A SHEPHERD, HE WILL CARE FOR HIS FLOCK, GATHERING THE LAMBS IN HIS ARMS, HUGGING THEM AS HE CARRIES THEM. (ISAIAH 40:11 MSG)

The Israelites weren't on their own, and you aren't on your own when you trust in God. One might think this pep talk would rally the troops and send them charging in to the Promised Land hootin' and hollerin'. But the rest of this story is going to knock your socks off.

Except for two fine young men named Joshua and Caleb, the Israelites basically said, "Forget it." They actually said to God and Moses that they wished they could go back and be slaves in Egypt rather than die at the hands of these giants and have their children taken into slavery. Yeah. Right. Like God was going to let that happen. C'mon, people.

God wasn't pleased with their response to his gracious promise—so make a note of that. Never settle for less than what he has in mind for you. When you do, you're allowing your fear and apprehension to hold you back. Hopefully, we're learning that we have a God who doesn't call us to live as though we just drew the short straw of life.

BY HIS MIGHTY POWER AT WORK WITHIN US, HE IS ABLE TO ACCOMPLISH INFINITELY MORE THAN WE WOULD EVER DARE TO ASK OR THINK. (EPHESIANS 3:20 NLT)

In response to Moses' encouragement, guess what they wanted to do? Get themselves a new leader who would take them back to—of all places—Egypt. Egypt, where they worked as slaves and were beaten by taskmasters.

They didn't draw the short straw. They grabbed it.

So God says, "If that's what you want, then turn around and head right back out to the desert and don't stop until you reach the Red Sea."

Now God had their attention. Somehow they must have thought he wasn't listening to all their crazy talk about going back to Egypt. Here's how they responded:

"What!? Back out to the desert? Oh, man..." (You can just imagine that was said with a whine.) "Do we *have* to? No, we blew it. We were wrong. We'll go back and fight just like you told us to. C'mon everybody! Grab your weapons! We've got some giants to slay."

But Moses said, "NO, NO, no. Not so fast. The Lord has told me he won't go with you now. You can't win. Don't go!"

What would you do?

Would you go?

Do you think they should have gone?

I don't, either.

But they went.

They lost.

Ever heard the term "stiff-necked people?"

They coined that phrase.

CHAPTER 6

SOMETIMES I FEEL DEFEATED

Emotions are a tricky business.

I know you've heard lots of times to listen to them and get in touch with them. That's not all bad. But remember, emotions can't always be trusted.

Emotions are real (hence the book), but not always reliable.

You may feel unloved. But God always loves you.

You may feel alone. But you'll never be forsaken.

You may feel inadequate. But God has graciously equipped you.

You may feel guilty. But your sins have been forgiven and forgotten.

You may feel your prayers have gone unheard. But you know that doesn't line up with God's promises.

The enemy loves messing with our heads. He's the father of all lies and his title is well earned. All he has to do is throw a defeating thought our way, and so often we have no trouble running with it, do we? Satan can take a long coffee break when we're doing all the work for him. And if we're feeling defeated then he's feeling victorious.

But we don't have to take this lying down. In fact, we're far from powerless so put on your boots.

WE TAKE CAPTIVE EVERY THOUGHT TO MAKE IT OBEDIENT TO CHRIST. (2 CORINTHIANS 10:5)

You are in control of your thoughts.

They don't have the power to run away *with* you or get the best *of* you. Understand that. They are in your control, and you are empowered to dismiss immediately any thought that doesn't line up with the truth that God has revealed. Want to get a handle on your unreliable emotions? Get a handle on your thoughts.

How exactly do we *capture* a thought and make it fall in line? That's not an easy concept but God has empowered you in a number of ways.

First of all, you can pray. When something's going on in your head, and you know it isn't right, immediately give it to God. Say something like, "Lord, this isn't from you. Please dismiss that thought from my head." Make a conscious effort to redirect your thinking.

Second, "garbage in, garbage out" applies to so many things in this world—your head included. Be careful about what you let in there.

BE CAREFUL WHAT YOU THINK, BECAUSE YOUR THOUGHTS RUN YOUR LIFE. (PROVERBS 4:23 NCV)

Hmmmmmm. No small things these thoughts of ours. They direct our actions and affect our emotions.

And you can say you're not influenced by these things, but it *matters* what you allow into your mind. If you've convinced yourself you're immune to your TV, podcast, music, and magazine choices, then Satan just threw a little victory confetti.

Third, make it your business to know what the truth is so you'll be equipped to recognize Satan's lies when he throws them your way. Don't be in the dark about this stuff.

Truth is found in your Bible.

Keep it at the top of your mind.

Turn to it.

Rest in it.

Cherish it.

Run to it.

Use it.

Use it as a weapon.

Victory always resides in the truth.

CHAPTER 7

SOMETIMES I FEEL HOPELESS

Name a vegetable. Any vegetable. Guaranteed it tastes better with a little salt. And where would potato chips, french fries, and popcorn be without it?

I ask you.

Clearly, no kitchen worth its salt would be without it. That could get ugly.

IS TASTELESS FOOD EATEN WITHOUT SALT? (JOB 6:6)

Salt takes the bland and makes it palatable and a bit more interesting. It brings the flavors of food to life. If food were black and white, salt would be the paintbrush that gave it rich, vibrant color.

And God says that we are salt. We are to add flavor to the world around us.

YOU MUST HAVE THE QUALITIES OF SALT AMONG YOURSELVES AND LIVE IN PEACE WITH EACH OTHER. (MARK 9:50 NLT)

God-given salt takes your personality and brings to life all the little treasures stored in your DNA. It makes you the person God created you to be. Your language, your choices, your emotions, your thoughts, and your priorities are all flavored by it.

LET YOUR CONVERSATION BE ALWAYS FULL OF GRACE, SEASONED WITH SALT, SO THAT YOU MAY KNOW HOW TO ANSWER EVERYONE. (COLOSSIANS 4:6)

Work should be done excellently when it's left up to you. Words should be more kind when they come out of your mouth. Needs should be met generously when it's up to you. Dealings should be done honestly when your name is on the dotted line.

Feeling good about all that? I hope so. However, sorry to rattle your saltshaker, but you have to know all that goodness isn't without its struggles. In fact, the struggles are often necessary to produce it.

EVERYONE WILL BE SALTED WITH FIRE. (MARK 9:49)

Ouch. No matter how many ways you try to read that, it just doesn't sound good, does it? But, by the sound of it, no one is going to escape—can you interpret the word *everyone* any other way? I couldn't either, and believe me, I tried.

Let's talk about that a bit. One minute we're putting salt on french fries and the next thing you know we're in a firestorm.

We all know what the firestorms of life are. We don't like them. They're our struggles and disappointments. They're the events and circumstances that make us sad and sometimes feel quite hopeless.

Certainly, no one wishes for such things. But can we learn to appreciate these struggles if we know they're producing the qualities of salt in us?

THOUGH YOU HAVE MADE ME SEE TROUBLES, MANY AND BITTER, YOU WILL RESTORE MY LIFE AGAIN; FROM THE DEPTHS OF THE EARTH YOU WILL AGAIN BRING ME UP. YOU WILL INCREASE MY HONOR AND COMFORT ME ONCE MORE. (PSALM 71:20-21)

With all this talk of salt and firestorms the promise in that verse could be missed. God will restore you—and that's why we have every reason to be hopeful. He won't leave you in the darkness.

And I hope you didn't miss the plan. God will increase your honor.

I'd say that's a verse worth spending some time with.

But notice there's an order in which God accomplishes all this in you:

First the struggle, then the honor.

God honors us with qualities that make the world wonder what's going on with us. At least that's his plan. He is very specific in Galatians 5 about what his spirit in us looks like. We are to be a people who possess love, joy, peace, patience, kindness, goodness, faithfulness, gentleness, and self-control.

That's some good stuff. It's the stuff your struggles produce. It's the stuff your reputation is made of, and you can't put a price on that.

A GOOD NAME IS MORE DESIRABLE THAN GREAT RICHES; TO BE ESTEEMED IS BETTER THAN SILVER OR GOLD. (PROVERBS 22:1)

Okay. Now that we know how all this works, here's some good news that most of the world never hears or understands. It's a zinger. Ready?

You can be joyful even in your hardships.

Yup.

What you just learned in this chapter can instill confidence, hope, and even joy when your world falls apart. It's not natural, of course, to welcome suffering and sadness. Nobody wants it. But we're asked to have an understanding of the part they play in making us the people God wants us to be.

WE ALSO HAVE JOY WITH OUR TROUBLES BECAUSE WE KNOW THAT THESE TROUBLES PRODUCE PATIENCE. AND PATIENCE PRODUCES CHARACTER, AND CHARACTER PRODUCES HOPE. (ROMANS 5:3-4 NCV)

Again, there's a sense of order in that process, isn't there? Trouble. Patience. Hope.

God has a plan.

And it's always a good one.

Rome wasn't built in a day, and neither were people of great character.

Hang in there with him.

Masterpieces like you take time.

FOR WE ARE GOD'S MASTERPIECES. HE HAS CREATED US ANEW IN CHRIST JESUS, SO THAT WE CAN DO THE GOOD THINGS HE PLANNED FOR US LONG AGO. (EPHESIANS 2:10 NLT)

CHAPTER 8

SOMETIMES I FEEL ORDINARY

YOU.

A masterpiece.

Do you buy that?

Can you grasp that you are indeed such a treasure?

Masterpieces are one of a kind—so rare and valuable that they're kept in high-security museums with video cameras and armed guards standing by 24/7. Understandable, since they can't be replaced. No duplicates exist. I suppose copies and imitations are made, but we don't value those very much, do we?

According to Webster's dictionary a *masterpiece* is—

**MAS•TER•PIECE |MASTƎR PĒSI N. I.
THE MOST OUTSTANDING WORK OF A
CREATIVE ARTIST OR CRAFTSMAN 2. AN
OUTSTANDING ACHIEVEMENT.**

You are outstanding. You could be in a big crowd, and your set of gifts, talents, and strengths would stand out. How could that be? You probably see yourself as someone who blends into a crowd pretty well. Maybe you feel you blend in so well you're actually indistinguishable from those around you. That's not such a great feeling, is it?

But you stand out because no one else in this universe (which consists of more than six billion people), or those who've lived before you, possess what makes you...you.

Hard to believe that? Don't make God small. Don't underestimate what he was doing when he chose the 46 chromosomes that became you. The best thing you can do is give your oh-so-special self back to him so he can use you for what he had in mind. You'll find God's plan for you is always better than your own, so keep in close touch with him on that.

Oh. And don't think he doesn't have a plan for your life. God had you figured out way before you made your first Christmas list.

In this light, doesn't it make you feel a little silly for ever wanting or trying to be like somebody else? First of all, you could only pull off a poor imitation of whoever you were attempting to be, and that surely isn't part of God's plan. Second of all, you could miss your own special gifts and talents while you're trying to prove you have ones you don't.

At times you may feel labeled and defined by the world. Your friends, your teachers, your dog, your grandma, and the mailman all have thoughts about you, and those thoughts may be very different. It can be confusing.

Those opinions can really throw us for a loop. They may have even given you the wrong idea about who you are and what you're capable of.

Let's get this straight: You are who you are because of who God is and how he made you—and that's some good news, my friend.

You are important.

THAT'S HOW MUCH YOU MEAN TO ME! THAT'S HOW MUCH I LOVE YOU! I'D SELL OFF THE WHOLE WORLD TO GET YOU BACK, TRADE THE CREATION JUST FOR YOU. (ISAIAH 43:4 MSG)

You are covered.

HIS HUGE OUTSTRETCHED ARMS PROTECT YOU—UNDER THEM YOU ARE PERFECTLY SAFE; HIS ARMS FEND OFF ALL HARM. (PSALM 91:4 MSG)

You are a winner.

FOR THE LORD TAKES DELIGHT IN HIS PEOPLE; HE CROWNS THE HUMBLE WITH VICTORY. (PSALM 149:4)

You are hopeful.

MAY THE GOD OF HOPE FILL YOU WITH ALL JOY AND PEACE AS YOU TRUST IN HIM, SO

THAT YOU MAY OVERFLOW WITH HOPE BY THE POWER OF THE HOLY SPIRIT. (ROMANS 15:13)

You are cared for.

THEN MY ENEMIES WILL TURN BACK WHEN I CALL FOR HELP. BY THIS I WILL KNOW THAT GOD IS FOR ME...IN GOD I TRUST AND AM NOT AFRAID. (PSALM 56:9-11)

You are peaceful.

YOU WILL KEEP IN PERFECT PEACE THOSE WHOSE MINDS ARE STEADFAST, BECAUSE THEY TRUST IN YOU. (ISAIAH 26:3)

You are championed.

GOD, WHO GOT YOU STARTED IN THIS SPIRITUAL ADVENTURE...WILL NEVER GIVE UP ON YOU. NEVER FORGET THAT. (1 CORINTHIANS 1:9 MSG)

You are lifted up.

YOU MAKE YOUR SAVING HELP MY SHIELD, AND YOUR RIGHT HAND SUSTAINS ME; YOUR HELP HAS MADE ME GREAT. (PSALM 18:35)

You are heard.

I POUR OUT BEFORE HIM MY COMPLAINT; BEFORE HIM I TELL MY TROUBLE. WHEN MY SPIRIT GROWS FAINT WITHIN ME, IT IS YOU WHO WATCH OVER MY WAY. (PSALM 142:2-3)

You are a treasure.

NOW IF YOU OBEY ME FULLY AND KEEP MY COVENANT, THEN OUT OF ALL NATIONS YOU WILL BE MY TREASURED POSSESSION. (EXODUS 19:5)

You are beautiful.

LET THE KING BE ENTHRALLED BY YOUR BEAUTY; HONOR HIM, FOR HE IS YOUR LORD. (PSALM 45:11)

You are unafraid.

SO DO NOT FEAR, FOR I AM WITH YOU; DO NOT BE DISMAYED, FOR I AM YOUR GOD. I WILL STRENGTHEN YOU AND HELP YOU; I WILL UPHOLD YOU WITH MY RIGHTEOUS RIGHT HAND. (ISAIAH 41:10)

You are found.

I WILL SEARCH FOR THE LOST AND BRING BACK THE STRAYS. I WILL BIND UP THE INJURED AND STRENGTHEN THE WEAK. (EZEKIEL 34:16)

You are God's.

SEE WHAT GREAT LOVE THE FATHER HAS LAVISHED ON US, THAT WE SHOULD BE CALLED CHILDREN OF GOD! AND THAT IS WHAT WE ARE! (1 JOHN 3:1)

You are unique.

BUT GOD HAD SPECIAL PLANS FOR ME
AND SET ME APART FOR HIS WORK EVEN
BEFORE I WAS BORN. (GALATIANS 1:15 NCV)

You are safe.

THE NAME OF THE Lord IS A FORTIFIED
TOWER; THE RIGHTEOUS RUN TO IT AND
ARE SAFE. (PROVERBS 18:10)

You are loved.

I HAVE LOVED YOU WITH AN EVERLASTING
LOVE; I HAVE DRAWN YOU WITH UNFAILING
KINDNESS. (JEREMIAH 31:3)

You are precious.

"DON'T BE AFRAID," HE SAID, "FOR YOU ARE
VERY PRECIOUS TO GOD. BE AT PEACE;
TAKE HEART AND BE STRONG!" (DANIEL
10:19 NLT)

And only you are you.

YOU'RE BLESSED WHEN YOU'RE CONTENT WITH JUST WHO YOU ARE—NO MORE, NO LESS. THAT'S THE MOMENT YOU FIND YOURSELVES PROUD OWNERS OF EVERYTHING THAT CAN'T BE BOUGHT. (MATTHEW 5:5 MSG)

CHAPTER 9

SOMETIMES I FEEL DISAPPOINTED

Masterpiece that you are, it doesn't mean life is always a bowl of cherries. (Why cherries represent everything cheery and right, I'm not sure. But I do know life is not always a bowl of them.)

We've talked about having joy in our struggles, but that doesn't mean we feel joyful all the time.

In fact, disappointment is one of the first emotions we experience. One minute you're floating in warm, safe water, and the next you're being swatted on the behind, wiped down, and handled by about a half-dozen pairs of hands. So what do you do?

You cry.

You cry, and everybody laughs and claps—including your mother. You understand the world right from the get-go, don't you?

Just when we seemingly have this disappointment thing all figured out, along comes this:

ANYONE WHO TRUSTS IN HIM WILL NEVER BE DISAPPOINTED. (1 PETER 2:6 NCV)

Never?

Did he say "never"?

Seriously.

He said "never."

Okay, so what do we do with the things in our lives that are by no other definition disappointments? An illness, a death, a dad who didn't parent you, a team you wanted to be part of, a friend you should have been able to trust, a test you couldn't pass, a college that didn't want you, or a mom who drank too much.

And then there's disappointment of global proportions. You didn't ask for a world haunted by war, hunger, and terrorist attacks.

Of course some disappointments in life are brought about by our own foolish mistakes. Our actions have consequences. *That we can understand*—we may not take joy in it, but at least it's logical to us.

The disappointments we don't ask for are harder to understand.

Either way, here's what we know: In times of our darkest disappointments God is at work. You can almost hear him calling your name. He's asking you to come close, real close, so close you can feel him, almost see him, rest in him, and oh, yes, trust in him. And then get out of his way because you're just a breath away from seeing God's glory shine in your life in unpredictable ways.

Know how I know that? Because he said so.

THEN YOU WILL KNOW THAT I AM THE LORD; THOSE WHO HOPE IN ME WILL NOT BE DISAPPOINTED. (ISAIAH 49:23)

Scripture says ultimately you're not going to be disappointed...or defeated.

HE WILL NOT LET YOU BE DEFEATED. (PSALM 121:3 NCV)

We get a little glimpse of what he's up to in Romans 8:28.

AND WE KNOW THAT IN ALL THINGS GOD WORKS FOR THE GOOD OF THOSE WHO LOVE HIM, WHO HAVE BEEN CALLED ACCORDING TO HIS PURPOSE. (ROMANS 8:28)

ALL things...never disappointed. Interesting how these verses don't leave a crack in the door for doubt to enter in. Too bad we so easily let it slip in through the window. We let it come on in, sit on our couch, eat our pretzels, play our video games, and spend the night.

God wants you to know for certain that nothing this world dishes out will get the best of you. You belong to him.

Scripture doesn't promise everything will make sense. God's reasons for doing things aren't always going to be clear. But that's okay. He's given us a heads-up on that one, too:

"MY THOUGHTS ARE NOTHING LIKE YOUR THOUGHTS," SAYS THE Lord. "AND MY WAYS ARE FAR BEYOND ANYTHING YOU COULD IMAGINE." (ISAIAH 55:8 NLT)

You and God don't always think alike. Your idea of disappointment may not be his. Sometimes God allows overwhelming circumstances if it means his will in your life is accomplished.

Trusting in God often means waiting on him. In fact, some translations of 1 Peter 2:6 say "those who wait on the Lord" and some say "those who trust in the Lord" will never be disappointed. Clearly, stamping our feet and demanding our own way isn't going to fly. Patience is required on our part. Being patient shapes us into people with character—and that's a good thing, isn't it?

Aren't you relieved it doesn't say only those who are well-educated will never be disappointed...or only the able-bodied, well-prepared, self-sufficient, strong, wealthy, righteous, good-looking, and talented?

Yeah, sometimes we place a great deal of importance in those things, but at the end of the day not one of them can instill true peace in our hearts and souls.

So I've got to let you know something pretty cool about those of us who are asked to wait on and put our hope in God. It was one of the reasons I was able to assure you something awesome is about to happen in your life.

**BUT THOSE WHO HOPE IN THE LORD WILL
RENEW THEIR STRENGTH. THEY WILL SOAR
ON WINGS LIKE EAGLES; THEY WILL RUN
AND NOT GROW WEARY, THEY WILL WALK
AND NOT BE FAINT. (ISAIAH 40:31)**

No small reward. Let's just say it's worth the wait.

No matter what your world looks or feels like at this moment, you can possess a peace and calmness that doesn't make a lick of sense to the world.

Why?

C'mon...

...you just heard it.

Not that long ago.

One page earlier.

Because you're trusting in the Lord. (I knew you knew that. I was just playin' with you.)

Give it a try.

Put your hand in the hand of Jesus and just see—but before you do, take a good, close look at it. You'll see it's pretty roughed up and scarred.

(That was for you.)

CHAPTER 10

SOMETIMES I FEEL UNNOTICED

Know what else is going on during your hard times and disappointments? More than you may have ever considered.

God is tracking it.

Literally.

Maybe God has a book or maybe he does the math in his head. Who knows? But all these sad times, struggles, and tears are not going unnoticed. God is paying close attention.

God doesn't call these times a "phase" or blame them on your hormones. God takes your sadness to heart. God remembers it and, as far as we know, has no intention of forgetting it. He'll forget our sins, but not our tears. How cool is that?

YOU KEEP TRACK OF ALL MY SORROWS. YOU HAVE COLLECTED ALL MY TEARS IN YOUR BOTTLE. YOU HAVE RECORDED EACH ONE IN YOUR BOOK. (PSALM 56:8 NLT)

Why? Maybe when we see God face-to-face he'll pull out the book of you and share with you what the Holy Spirit accomplished through your pain.

God cares about you at such a deep level and loves you so fully that not a single tear escapes his notice.

GOD KEEPS AN EYE ON HIS FRIENDS, HIS EARS PICK UP EVERY MOAN AND GROAN. (PSALM 34:15 MSG)

God hears your faintest sigh. Now *that is* being noticed. He hears it and understands its meaning. Now *that is* being understood.

HE MADE THEIR HEARTS, SO HE UNDERSTANDS EVERYTHING THEY DO. (PSALM 33:15 NLT)

Friends are great, but they don't know your whole heart. Talk to God just the way you talk to your friends. Anytime, anywhere, for as long as you want. You have God's undivided, wholehearted, take-the-phone-off-the-hook-because-nothing-is-more-important-than-what-my-child-has-to-say attention.

More on that in the next chapter.

CHAPTER 11

SOMETIMES I FEEL INEFFECTIVE

Prayer puts the wheels of heaven in motion. Does it blow your mind just a bit that something so small as a quiet conversation originating from little ol' you on little ol' planet Earth can impact anything at all, much less the heart of your Heavenly Father?

Yup. Eternity can change in an instant...before you even say "amen." Here's how I know that:

THE MOMENT YOU [DANIEL] BEGAN PRAYING A COMMAND WAS GIVEN. I AM HERE TO TELL YOU WHAT IT WAS, FOR YOU ARE VERY PRECIOUS TO GOD. (DANIEL 9:23 NLT)

Wheels aren't set in motion casually. Wheels turn because Almighty God gives a command. Those commands are often given as a result of prayer.

James can't say it much more clearly, can he?

THE PRAYER OF A RIGHTEOUS PERSON IS POWERFUL AND EFFECTIVE. (JAMES 5:16)

It doesn't say *sometimes* your prayers are powerful and effective. Let the meaning of that settle in. When you pray, great things happen.

So, do you wonder where the fireworks, parties, awards, acclaim, and other great things are, for heaven's sake? We all feel unheard at times, so what's up with that?

First, you may be asking for something that is simply, irrevocably not in God's plan for you. That doesn't mean he is preventing great things from happening for you. It means your gracious Heavenly Father is clearing the path for his plans—so don't take your ball and go home. In your oh-so-earthly way you may have had an idea that wasn't so hot. If that's the case, aren't you glad he's looking out for you?

Second, your timing may be just a tad off. Maybe God's answer is: "Sure, I'd love to give, take away, expand, develop, increase, open up, whatever you may be petitioning for. But...not right now." If that's the case, have a seat.

Third, God may be answering you in a way you can't see.

TRULY, O GOD OF ISRAEL, OUR SAVIOR, YOU WORK IN MYSTERIOUS WAYS. (ISAIAH 45:15)

It's true. Could be God's setting the stage, arranging the circumstances, and creating the agenda that'll bring about your answer in a fashion that's in line with God's will for you. If that's the case, get out of the way.

Fourth, sometimes God's answer is "no." What are you gonna do? It's always about God's will, not yours—right? If that's the case, trust him. If the Father could say no to Jesus in the Garden of Gethsemane (Matthew 26:36–42), I guess we should expect a "no" on occasion to our requests as well. It's all about doing what's best for us and accomplishing God's will in this world.

Whatever the case may be, don't neglect your prayer time. Know what can happen when you do that?

YOU DO NOT HAVE BECAUSE YOU DO NOT ASK GOD. (JAMES 4:2)

Now that's a crying shame, isn't it? Don't miss out on one ounce of the Lord's goodness just because you got a little too busy.

Did you know Jesus would often go away all by himself to talk to his Father? Sometimes he would spend all night in prayer. I'm thinking if he felt the need to stay in such close contact, we probably shouldn't ignore our own need for it.

A little prayer time can save you a whole lot of time trying to figure out your own solutions to your problems. It also means you're never powerless over situations that seem hopeless.

We know what we have to do, but how do we do it? How do we pray? It's not the first time that question has been asked. Even the disciples asked Jesus how to pray.

Moses gave us a great example.

THE Lord WOULD SPEAK TO MOSES FACE TO FACE, AS ONE SPEAKS TO A FRIEND. (EXODUS 33:11)

Doesn't sound so hard, does it? We know how to do that, don't we? We've talked face-to-face with friends since we were old enough to have play dates.

Don't think you need to be a Moses to talk to the Lord as a friend. Moses, Tom, Dick, Harry, Sally, Sue...the offer is all the same:

"LOOK! I STAND AT THE DOOR AND KNOCK. IF YOU HEAR MY VOICE AND OPEN THE DOOR, I WILL COME IN, AND WE WILL SHARE A MEAL AS FRIENDS." (REVELATION 3:20 NLT)

How often do you hear a shout from Jesus? Really, not that often. But did you catch his raised voice? It was in that exclamation point after the word *Look*. He's saying, *Don't overlook me*. Why? Because if you do, you'll miss out on so much fun. Let Jesus in. He's not coming in to lecture, condemn, bully, boss around, or complain. He wants to sit down and share a little something to eat with you. As a friend. That's prayer.

A God who's close and ready to listen isn't a common perception for those who don't know him well. Unfortunately, this misguided notion of a faraway, judgmental, hard-to-please-but-you-better-try kind of God persists. That's not our God. We know this because we've experienced his love. And we don't have to take anyone's word on that.

God's looking for the kind of RSVP David gave him in Psalm 27:8:

MY HEART HAS HEARD YOU SAY, "COME AND TALK WITH ME." AND MY HEART RESPONDS "LORD, I AM COMING." (PSALM 27:8 NLT)

Does God really want to hear from me? All the details of my life—as ridiculous and boring as they may be at times? Does he really want to be loaded down with what makes me sad and hear about my embarrassing moments?

Well, find out.

Set aside some time.

Set aside a place.

Set aside your own agenda.

You've got an invitation to lunch.

CHAPTER 12

SOMETIMES I FEEL WEAK

Here it is.

It's the no-sex-'til-you're-married chapter.

It's the but-everybody's-doin'-it chapter.

It's the but-how-else-will-I-know-if-he/she-loves-me chapter.

It's the that's-not-really-sex-is-it? chapter.

I bet I have your attention. Just guessing.

A lot of people want your attention. Marketing executives strategize with this *you gotta have this to be cool and sexy* message.

You can't help it.

You see it, you hear it, and before you know it, you're caught up in it.

Satan will use any opportunity to trip you up. Billboards, music videos, song lyrics, movies, Web sites, you name it... He's got all kinds of lies about what makes you cool and sexy, and he is an expert at making you believe them.

KEEP A COOL HEAD. STAY ALERT. THE DEVIL IS POISED TO POUNCE, AND WOULD LIKE NOTHING BETTER THAN TO CATCH YOU NAPPING. KEEP YOUR GUARD UP. (1 PETER 5:8 MSG)

Rub your eyes and get a double espresso if you need to. We've been put on high-alert status. Actions are preceded by thoughts, which is why your thought life in this area is something to keep in check.

ABOVE ALL ELSE, GUARD YOUR HEART, FOR EVERYTHING YOU DO FLOWS FROM IT. (PROVERBS 4:23)

You don't have to look any farther than your television after 8 p.m. to understand why it's easy to get sleepy and let down your guard. We've got beautiful people with cool jobs who live in hip apartments and wear clothes we'd all be proud to hang in our closets. The places they go, the things they do, the partners they have—it all looks so harmless. In fact, more than that, they all seem to lead glamorous lives that can make us feel dull and ordinary.

Ohhhh, that's right—I just remembered—they're not *real* people. They're people with a team of writers, stylists, set decorators, and personal trainers behind them.

Real people who play with fire get burned. You have casual sexual relationships, and you have babies, diseases, and emotional upheaval that'll make witty comebacks the last thing you're capable of pulling off.

If God messed around with this message, we wouldn't take it so seriously, but the truth is, God tells it like it is whether we like it or not.

Think he should lighten up? Just a little bit? When it comes to your safety (and that means your physical and emotional safety) your Heavenly Father doesn't write with gray ink. It's a black-and-white deal.

BUT DON'T FORGET, HE'S ALSO A RESPONSIBLE FATHER WHO WON'T LET YOU GET BY WITH SLOPPY LIVING. YOUR LIFE IS A JOURNEY YOU MUST TRAVEL WITH A DEEP CONSCIOUSNESS OF GOD. (1 PETER 1:17-18 MSG)

Our Father gives us boundaries so he can take care of us. He has respect for you and demands that same respect from others in your life. He demands no less from you. So what exactly does that look like?

You may have to go home when you want to stay.

You may have to hang out with friends when you'd rather be alone with your date.

You may have to turn off the TV when you want to watch it.

You may have to delete instead of click.

You may have to set boundaries when you don't want to hold back.

You may have to say "no" when you want to say "yes."

KEEP YOURSELVES FROM SEXUAL PROMISCUITY. LEARN TO APPRECIATE AND GIVE DIGNITY TO YOUR BODY. (1 THESSALONIANS 4:3-4 MSG)

God actually is the author of all fun stuff—just in case you doubt that a little bit right now. He's not looking to sentence you to weekends of research at the library or to Canasta games with your grandma. (Not that there's anything wrong with that.) But he knows how much fun you can have when you're not carrying all the baggage that comes from messing around with premarital sex. Trust him on this one.

LIVE CAREFREE BEFORE GOD; HE IS MOST CAREFUL WITH YOU. (1 PETER 5:7 MSG)

Listen, sex is beautiful.

Sex is ordained by God.

Sanctioned by God.

Is a gift from God.

But only within the parameters of marriage.

If you're not married, you're not permitted to have sex. Period. Is it difficult? Sure. But it's the only definition of safe sex that God uses.

So take a stand. This is no time to be a wimp, my young, hormonal friend. "No" is a valid response.

I DON'T KNOW ABOUT YOU, BUT I'M RUNNING HARD FOR THE FINISH LINE. I'M GIVING IT EVERYTHING I'VE GOT. NO SLOPPY LIVING FOR ME! (1 CORINTHIANS 9:26 MSG)

If you've already crossed that no-sex line and are feeling defeated in any way, shape, or form, then go directly back to Chapter 2.

Defeat and guilt are not the messages here. It's about freedom. Then reread Chapter 3 and remember you can't exhaust God's grace.

Now go have some fun.

CHAPTER 13

SOMETIMES I FEEL WORTHLESS

Come with me to John 8. I have a woman I want you to meet.

She was used—in so many ways was she used. She was used by men and she was used as a political pawn. And hey, if she got killed in the process, who cared?

To the Pharisees she was expendable.

To *almost* everyone she was worthless.

She may have slept around. We can't be sure, but somehow she got herself cast in the lead role of a scheme orchestrated by the religious leaders. Here is what happened: This woman was caught in bed with a man who wasn't her husband—and probably not by chance. The scene had to have witnesses—at least two. The punishment for her actions was death, so more than accusatory hearsay was required. Now the likelihood of having several witnesses in a bedroom at just the right moment isn't all that great.

So you can just imagine these Pharisees plotting their scheme, sneaking around in some bedroom, waiting for just the right moment to pop out of nowhere with one big *gotcha!*

And where was her partner? He was due the same punishment but apparently, her accusers let him go. One doesn't have to go too far out on a limb to conjecture that this event just may have been a setup.

Who's the sleazebag here?

The Pharisees couldn't drag her in front of Jesus fast enough. Not because they couldn't wait for justice to be served. Oh, no. But because they wanted Jesus to mess up. Jesus was a little too popular and wielding a bit too much authority for their taste. That's what this was all about—the undoing of Jesus' authority.

Very briefly: The law of Moses would've handled this situation one way and Roman law another. So whichever way Jesus ruled, they were going to nail him for ignoring one law or the other.

End of background.

Beginning of story.

And what a story. This has to be one of the most precious moments in all of the New Testament.

These religious leaders weren't exactly steeped in compassion. So instead of bringing the woman to Jesus in private, they interrupted a gathering of people listening to Jesus teach. Based on history, one would assume Jesus never attracted a small crowd, so this was an opportune moment for humiliation—first for the woman and then for Jesus.

And a moment of triumph for the Pharisees.

So the Pharisees brought her to Jesus.

Jesus was quiet.

I'm sure they were thinking, *He's absolutely confounded.*

Actually, it didn't appear Jesus was making eye contact with anybody because he was writing in the dirt.

What I wouldn't give to know the words his fingers were forming.

The Pharisees kept at him. They weren't leaving until he played their game.

Finally, Jesus spoke. These have become pretty famous words, haven't they?

"LET ANY ONE OF YOU WHO IS WITHOUT SIN BE THE FIRST TO THROW A STONE AT HER." (JOHN 8:7)

And then Jesus went back to his writing. In fact, he kept writing while his words were sinking in and their defeat was becoming clear.

One by one they slinked away. The ones with the most to lose went first. Funny how those humiliation tables have a way of being turned.

Wouldn't you love to hear their grumbling as they made their way back to their homes?

Jesus was still writing, by the way. He didn't stop until it was just him and her. Then he looked into the face of this broken soul and probably saw the fear in her eyes. Maybe she was wondering if there wasn't just one accuser left behind who could hurl a rock squarely at her head.

But it was just Jesus and her.

He spoke first.

"Where are they? Has no one condemned you?"

"No one, sir," she said.

And now comes the moment that takes this death-defying afternoon and turns it into the very definition of the grace of God.

"Then neither do I condemn you," Jesus declared.

It was this grace that gave her back her self-esteem.

It was this grace that allowed her to see herself differently.

It was this grace that allowed her to forgive herself.

It was this grace that lifted her head.

And yours.

BUT YOU, Lord, ARE A SHIELD AROUND ME, MY GLORY, AND THE ONE WHO LIFTS MY HEAD HIGH. (PSALM 3:3)

Jesus was her shield against every stone, and he's your shield, too. Most of us have probably felt at some time or another as though there were a few stones in the air ready to bean us from behind.

But we have a defender. And there's no enemy who can outwit him.

Jesus' grace didn't indicate his approval. He didn't say her sin was acceptable—but her sin didn't make her unacceptable.

Sin never gets in the way of his love.

And when Jesus is the rock you're standing on, you don't have to worry about the ones the world is ready to throw.

BE MY ROCK OF REFUGE, TO WHICH I CAN ALWAYS GO; GIVE THE COMMAND TO SAVE ME, FOR YOU ARE MY ROCK AND MY FORTRESS. (PSALM 71:3)

CHAPTER 14

SOMETIMES I FEEL LIKE A LOSER

We've all been there.

Loserhood isn't a new concept.

Come with me to a place called Bethesda in the year 30 AD (give or take a few months). We're going to the pool because the main character of our story spends a lot of time there. (See John 5.)

He's all alone. Part of a crowd but all alone. Unable to walk, he's lived 38 years in a horizontal position.

So what would bring a man who can't swim to the pool, you ask? Well, every so often the water in this pool swirls, and the belief is that the first one in will be healed. That means one winner and lots of losers—and this poor man always finds himself among the latter. Along with his limited abilities, he has no family or friends to help him into the pool.

So life goes on. On his mat.

And he's not hanging out poolside at the Bethesda Hilton. There are no cabanas or pink drinks with umbrellas being served by wait staff. Nor is it a hustling, bustling wing of the local hospital where doctors, nurses, pills, tubes, and machines are making everybody a bit more comfortable. It's really a mass of people at the ends of frayed and failing ropes. Ever feel like you'd fit right in at this pool party?

Are we surprised to find Jesus here? We shouldn't be.

He's in town for a feast, so he stops by. Our friend on the mat doesn't ask Jesus to heal him because he has no idea who Jesus is.

Our friend does know that this day is a bit different, though. His whole life has been spent watching ankles pass him by, but today somebody sits down beside him and asks him how he's doing. He speaks and someone listens. That's enough right there to put this day in the better-than-most category.

Jesus listens, but then he has something to say:

"GET UP! PICK UP YOUR MAT AND WALK." (JOHN 5:8)

Can't you just hear the man's response?

"Yeah, right. Listen, mister, if I could pick up my mat, do you think I'd be...whoa." There was simply no choice in the matter—this guy had to move.

Interestingly, both Jesus AND the guy on the mat got in trouble with the religious leaders. First, they scolded the crippled man for carrying his mat on the Sabbath. Then they got on Jesus' case for healing someone on the Sabbath. I know. You'd want to laugh if it wasn't so pathetic.

Jesus told them to stuff a sock in it. No, he didn't say that, but he did defend himself and, quite honestly, he had very little patience for the attitude of these "religious" leaders. Jesus said his Father works straight through, even on the Sabbath, and he does, too. And then it got really good: He went on to say that he'd be doing far greater things than healing this man—astonishing things.

Isn't that just the kind of God you want? A God who does astonishing things for those he loves?

So, if you're lying around on a mat and want to dance—ask him. Jesus changes lives.

YOU CHANGED MY SORROW INTO DANCING. YOU TOOK AWAY MY CLOTHES OF SADNESS AND CLOTHED ME IN HAPPINESS. (PSALM 30:11 NCV)

Stay tuned (or just turn the page) for more details—and new clothes.

CHAPTER 15

SOMETIMES I FEEL INADEQUATE

Looking to get off your mat, are you? Ready to start dancing down the street of life? Life can be quite the ball with the right dance partner.

Let God lead.

IN KINDNESS HE TAKES US FIRMLY BY THE HAND AND LEADS US INTO A RADICAL LIFE-CHANGE. (ROMANS 2:4 MSG)

And just see where you go.

ATTENTION TO GOD LEADS US OUT INTO THE OPEN, INTO A SPACIOUS, FREE LIFE. (ROMANS 8:6 MSG)

Radical, spacious, free. Yeah, we're liking the sound of that. Better than humdrum, suffocated, and confined, for crying out loud. But just how do we achieve such a life?

You can't.

You don't have the tools.

Never will.

Before you throw up your hands, throw in the towel, or throw down a pint of Ben and Jerry's, let me redirect your thinking. This inadequacy of ours is, in reality, quite freeing.

You're not left to your own devices because you don't have any. It'll never be your job to accomplish all the cool things the Lord has planned for you. It'll only be your job to open your heart and let the Holy Spirit accomplish all these cool things in and through you. We know better than to get too impressed with our very own inadequate selves, right?

BUT WE HAVE THIS TREASURE IN JARS OF CLAY TO SHOW THAT THIS ALL-SURPASSING POWER IS FROM GOD AND NOT FROM US. (2 CORINTHIANS 4:7)

Can I get an *Oh-thank-God-because-I-didn't-know-how-I-was-ever-going-to-pull-that-off-on-my-own* from somebody?

Any part of your life you try to keep control of is a piece of yourself you've withheld from God. That piece of you will never realize its full potential. The best thing to do is totally surrender everything you have. You do that very simply. You pray.

It can be as simple as: *Lord, I surrender my will to yours. Use me. Use my hands, my feet, my words, my mind, my relationships, my talents, my weaknesses, my car, my goldfish, my naturally curly hair. It's yours.*

Now what? What might a surrendered life look like? It can look like a lot of things—but inadequate isn't one of them.

You may shine a little brighter.

THOSE WHO ARE WISE WILL SHINE LIKE THE BRIGHTNESS OF THE HEAVENS, AND THOSE WHO LEAD MANY TO RIGHTEOUSNESS, LIKE THE STARS FOR EVER AND EVER. (DANIEL 12:3)

You may feel a little more secure.

HE WILL NOT LET YOUR FOOT SLIP—HE WHO WATCHES OVER YOU WILL NOT SLUMBER. (PSALM 121:3)

You may be a little more confident.

WITH YOUR HELP I CAN ADVANCE AGAINST A TROOP; WITH MY GOD I CAN SCALE A WALL. (2 SAMUEL 22:30)

You may kick up your heels a little more often.

BUT FOR YOU WHO REVERE MY NAME, THE SUN OF RIGHTEOUSNESS WILL RISE WITH HEALING IN ITS RAYS. AND YOU WILL GO OUT AND FROLIC LIKE WELL-FED CALVES. (MALACHI 4:2)

You may dream a little bigger.

EVERYTHING IS POSSIBLE FOR ONE WHO BELIEVES. (MARK 9:23)

CHAPTER 16

SOMETIMES I FEEL CONFUSED

So, you're dancing. Ever feel afraid you'll have two left feet? Miss a beat? Dance with the wrong partner? To the wrong song? Forget the steps? Have we had it with this metaphor? Sorry.

But, here's the point: To keep in step you have to hear the right music.

That's where the Bible comes in.

The Bible is one way God talks to you. There is a sense of interaction as you read it. Interaction with God. You talking to him. Him talking to you.

If you don't have a Bible, get one. Now, you do have to open it if you want this to work.

So put those shoes on your feet and take 'em for a spin. In other words, crack that Bible open and start reading. Before you do, ask God to bless you with understanding as you read. Ask for a focused mind and an open heart so you can hear what he has to say to you.

This can be a very personal, intimate activity. Once you start you'll be hooked. It'll become a marvelous discovery of what you need to hear.

Every day you read your Bible isn't going to bring mind-boggling revelations. In fact, there will be days when you wonder why you even bothered. But keep at it. What you're doing is deepening your relationship with God. All relationships take time—so invest as much as you can in this one.

Here are a few things to keep in mind while you read:

We believe the Bible appears just as the Lord intended it. It is his word without error. Human hands wrote it but not with their own insight.

Reading God's Word safeguards your heart and mind. That's important, because there are a lot of folks out there who'd love to dance with you but don't know their two left feet from a hole in the ground. You've been around long enough to know how many ideas are flying around out there in the name of religion and spirituality. There are even parts of the Bible that seem confusing. But our God is not a God of confusion. He gives us the ability to discern his message from false ones.

My sheep listen to my voice; I know them, and they follow me. (John 10:27)

It's not so easy for those who've said "no" to Jesus.

THE WORLD CANNOT ACCEPT HIM BECAUSE IT NEITHER SEES HIM NOR KNOWS HIM. BUT YOU KNOW HIM, FOR HE LIVES WITH YOU AND WILL BE IN YOU. (JOHN 14:17)

Ever heard of a plumb line? Carpenters use it to make sure they build structures that are square (not crooked). A plumb line hangs perfectly straight from top to bottom. So imagine God's Word as a plumb line. You know where you'll find Satan's falsehoods?

Sitting far off to the left or the right of that plumb line?

Nope.

As close to that perfectly straight line as possible. Oh, Satan's lies will seem almost believable. They may even sound pretty good. But, my friend, therein lies the trap. Satan is so good at making lies sound like the truth. And trust me, he has a lot of people fooled.

Paul warned us about them.

FOR SUCH PERSONS ARE FALSE APOSTLES, DECEITFUL WORKERS, MASQUERADING AS APOSTLES OF CHRIST. AND NO WONDER, FOR SATAN HIMSELF MASQUERADES AS AN ANGEL OF LIGHT. (2 CORINTHIANS 11:13-14)

But you won't be fooled when you're dancing with Jesus and know what's going on in that Bible of yours.

No twirling to the wrong music for you.

Now that we have that settled I will officially put an end to this metaphor.

CHAPTER 17

SOMETIMES I FEEL UNAPPEALING

Did you catch in that last chapter what John said about the Holy Spirit coming to live inside us? (John 14:17) That's a powerful concept that we simply have to try to understand the best we can.

Now, it only stands to reason that if God's Holy Spirit is there inhabiting your heart, he's not going to stay hidden there. Hide God? Not likely. Whatever's in your heart will show up on your face.

Of course, we're going to continue to have our crabby, less-than-pleasant moments. But overall your face can tell a story about the one to whom you belong.

SO OUR FACES ARE NOT COVERED. THEY SHOW THE BRIGHT GLORY OF THE LORD, AS THE LORD'S SPIRIT MAKES US MORE AND MORE LIKE OUR GLORIOUS LORD. (2 CORINTHIANS 3:18 CEV)

Reflecting God's glory.

In fact, brightly reflecting God's glory.

Apparently, God does not intend for us to be dull, dimly lit bulbs. It's also clear that as we grow in our relationship with God, we'll start looking more and more like him. His goal is to change you and then change you some more.

Remember, God started this work in us, and he isn't finished with us until we get to heaven. These changes are taking place in every aspect of who we are. You really aren't getting older; you're getting better. (I stole that from a hair-color commercial.)

Most likely you won't see this change in yourself. It's not meant to give you a boost as you brush your teeth or catch your reflection at the mall. God's glory is present in you to give honor to the One who put it there.

Moses asked to actually witness the fullness of God's glory, and Moses received all that he could handle. God covered Moses' eyes and passed by. Moses was only allowed to see God's back.

Understand we humans have no reference for this glory and brightness because it reflects God's holiness and righteousness. God's glory is not of this world, and we're not going to see it in all its fullness in this world. The only hint of its intensity is that heaven won't need another single source of light because of it. It's awesome. We'll leave it at that.

But, c'mon. *This* in *us*? It baffles the mind, doesn't it? But if it weren't so, God wouldn't have told us. So we count on it. It makes you far from unappealing.

THOSE WHO LOOK TO HIM ARE RADIANT; THEIR FACES ARE NEVER COVERED WITH SHAME. (PSALM 34:5)

By definition *radiance* and *joy* go hand in hand.

ra•di•ance |rā-dē-ān(t)s| n. 1. joy, energy, or good health discernible in somebody's face or demeanor 2. bright or glowing light

Synonyms for radiance are just as much fun: *Happiness, sparkle, glow, vivacity.*

Now go try to find that stuff in a face cream or a vitamin.

CHAPTER 18

SOMETIMES I FEEL WEARY

Most of us really aren't looking to break a sweat as we make our way through this world. We want our chosen paths to be level, pleasant, and void of rough terrain, right? Because when life requires a walking stick and a backpack, we get a little tired. We get weary from the journey. Sometimes our backpacks get so heavy we can hardly get out of bed to face another day of dragging that thing around the mountain one more time.

God describes what's going on during these times in the book of Jeremiah.

MY PEOPLE HAVE BEEN LOST SHEEP; THEIR SHEPHERDS HAVE LED THEM ASTRAY AND CAUSED THEM TO ROAM ON THE MOUNTAINS. THEY WANDERED OVER MOUNTAIN AND HILL AND FORGOT THEIR OWN RESTING PLACE. (JEREMIAH 50:6)

There are struggles God allows and uses in our lives. We've covered those. This isn't what we're talking about here. We're talking about the times we forget where our own resting place is.

When we forget a thing as important as this we can create steep mountains we were never intended to climb and loads we were never intended to carry. Can you imagine trudging down a difficult path for so long you actually *forget* life doesn't have to be so hard?

We get to a point where we accept our burdens and difficulties as a way of life. Hanging on to what we should let go of can easily become a mission.

Time for a time-out on the dusty trail. Have a seat on your backpack. Take a drink; I bet you're thirsty. Sit still for just a minute—at least long enough to let these next pages remind you of something I'm quite sure you already know.

Weariness is not from God. Weariness is our doing. There's a difference between working hard and persevering through the struggle versus running your anxious, worrisome self into the ground.

And we're all guilty of it.

Sometimes we tell our Heavenly Trail Guide we feel more suited for the job than he is. And then there are those times our Guide doesn't move fast enough, so we leave him by the side of the road and take the itinerary into our own hands. Which, by the way, God allows us to do. God honors our choices.

Sometimes we choose paths that look like so much fun. We see them and don't think twice. We don't consider the consequences or the twists and turns down those roads. They simply appeal to us, and we figure we only go around once, right?

Then before you know it, your boots weigh 50 pounds and your backpack is giving you a pain. You can't even remember what's in there anymore, but if you had to bet, you'd say it was a bunch of rocks. And you swear you had a good reason for choosing this route. But even that seems a little fuzzy about now. So how does one avoid chiropractic bills and blistered feet?

MY CHILD, USE COMMON SENSE AND SOUND JUDGMENT! ALWAYS KEEP THEM IN MIND. THEY WILL HELP YOU TO LIVE A LONG AND BEAUTIFUL LIFE. YOU WILL WALK SAFELY AND NEVER STUMBLE; YOU WILL REST WITHOUT A WORRY AND SLEEP SOUNDLY. (PROVERBS 3:21-24 CEV)

There was a treasure map in that verse. Did you see it? Go back and look again if it didn't pop out at you. Here's a clue—well maybe two: *common sense* and *sound judgment*. Hmm...common sense...sound judgment. Sounds like wisdom. Yup. A little check in at Proverbs lets us know we just may be on to something.

I INSTRUCT YOU IN THE WAY OF WISDOM AND LEAD YOU ALONG STRAIGHT PATHS. WHEN YOU WALK, YOUR STEPS WILL NOT BE HAMPERED; WHEN YOU RUN, YOU WILL NOT STUMBLE. (PROVERBS 4:11-12)

Don't you love that it doesn't say *walk, lumber,* or *saunter*? A life guided by wisdom is a strong one—capable of running without falling.

Are you wishing you'd known that before you found yourself with pebbles in your hiking boots and carrying a 50-pound backpack?

No matter how far off the course you are, you're never too far for God to lead you back. You know that. If it's wisdom you need, then wisdom is yours for the asking.

IF ANY OF YOU LACKS WISDOM, YOU SHOULD ASK GOD, WHO GIVES GENEROUSLY TO ALL WITHOUT FINDING FAULT, AND IT WILL BE GIVEN TO YOU. (JAMES 1:5)

Without finding fault means God will never say you're wrong for asking. Once you've come to him for help, he's never going to make you feel like a blockhead for the ways you messed up. You expect a little "I told you so," don't you? Sure, you'd appreciate it if it wasn't shouted from a mountaintop, but you expect maybe a little whisper in your ear. You at least have that coming, don't you? Well, yes, you do. But you won't get it. Wow. That is what we call mercy, my friend.

When you belong to him, he is on your side and, truly, he throws a party—and all the angels sing—when a lost backpacker is found in the woods and brought home again.

PROMISES FOR THE BACKPACKER:

1. No matter how heavy the backpack, God will carry it for you. "Come to me all you who are weary and burdened, and I will give you rest." (Matthew 11:28)

2. Against the greatest odds, God will give you strength. "He gives strength to the weary and increases the power of the weak." (Isaiah 40:29)

3. Amid the roughest terrain God will give you agility and a good pair of boots. "The Lord God is my strength. He makes me like a deer that does not stumble so I can walk on the steep mountains." (Habakkuk 3:19 NCV)

4. And God will give you company for the journey. "You were all called to travel on the same road and in the same direction, so stay together, both outwardly and inwardly." (Ephesians 4:4 MSG)

Outwardly and *inwardly*. Stick together in body and in spirit.

We stay strong that way.

We're happiest that way.

And God loves to see happy campers.

CHAPTER 19

SOMETIMES I FEEL FRAZZLED

A simple chapter.

Three word sentences.

Couldn't do two.

But never did four.

Take a break.

Take a breath.

Because life doesn't always have to be that hard.

Be unconditionally kind.

"Remind the people...to be peaceable and considerate, and always be gentle toward everyone." (Titus 3:1-2)

Live life simply.

"Give me neither poverty nor riches, but give me only my daily bread." (Proverbs 30:8)

Be a winner.

"Through their faith they defeated kingdoms. They did what was right, received God's promises and shut the mouths of lions." (Hebrews 11:33 NCV)

Sit still sometimes.

"In repentance and rest is your salvation, in quietness and trust is your strength." (Isaiah 30:15)

Follow your dreams.

"Hope deferred makes the heart sick, but a longing fulfilled is a tree of life." (Proverbs 13:12)

Set lofty goals.

"By his mighty power at work within us, he is able to accomplish infinitely more than we would ever dare to ask or think." (Ephesians 3:20 NLT)

Learn from mistakes.

"No discipline seems pleasant at the time, but painful. Later on, however, it produces a harvest of righteousness and peace for those who have been trained by it." (Hebrews 12:11).

Keep your promises.

"God can't stomach liars; he loves the company of those who keep their word." (Proverbs 12:22 MSG)

Sing a song.

"Satisfy us in the morning with your unfailing love, that we may sing for joy and be glad all our days." (Psalm 90:14)

Say nice things.

"Do not let any unwholesome talk come out of your mouths, but only what is helpful for building others up according to their needs, that it may benefit those who listen." (Ephesians 4:29)

Laugh a lot.

"Let the smile of your face shine on us, LORD. You have given me greater joy than those who have abundant harvests of grain and wine." (Psalm 4:6-7 NLT)

Share your stuff.

"Suppose a brother or sister is without clothes and daily food. If one of you says to them, 'Go in peace; keep warm and well fed' but does nothing about their physical needs, what good is it?" (James 2:15-16)

Ask for it.

"Ask and you will receive, and your joy will be complete." (John 16:24)

Keep on goin'.

"We are surrounded by a great cloud of people whose lives tell us what faith means. So let us run the race that is before us and never give up." (Hebrews 12:1 NCV)

Choose friends wisely.

"Young people...with wild friends bring shame to their parents." (Proverbs 28:7 NLT)

Expect good things.

"The LORD will guide you always; he will satisfy your needs in a sun-scorched land and will strengthen your frame. You will be like a well-watered garden, like a spring whose waters never fail." (Isaiah 58:11)

Ask for help.

"Pride leads to conflict; those who take advice are wise." (Proverbs 13:10 NLT)

Love your work.

"God wants all people to eat and drink and be happy in their work, which are gifts from God." (Ecclesiastes 3:13 NCV)

Think good thoughts.

"Finally, brothers and sisters, whatever is true, whatever is noble, whatever is right, whatever is pure, whatever is lovely, whatever is admirable—if anything is excellent or praiseworthy—think about such things." (Philippians 4:8)

Plan your future.

"The prudent understand where they are going, but fools deceive themselves." (Proverbs 14:8 NLT)

Get your rest.

"In peace I will lie down and sleep, for you alone, LORD, make me dwell in safety." (Psalm 4:8)

Say your prayers.

"When a believing person prays, great things happen." (James 5:16 NCV)

CHAPTER 20

SOMETIMES I FEEL TEMPTED

I want you to picture yourself in your ultimate comfort zone. Where are you? Maybe hanging out in your room, or sitting in your backyard, or driving in your car. Maybe you're reading, talking to a friend, listening to music, singing at the top of your lungs.

You catch sight of something out of the corner of your eye. You blink a couple of times. You continue to check it out and talk yourself out of what you're seeing. You shake your head a few times. *C'mon, man, no way. That is NOT a lion in my bedroom* (or car or wherever this thought took you).

It's not a pet lion (even if there is such a thing, this guy isn't it). It's a freaky, scary, hungry, mad, I'm-gonna-show-you-my-teeth-and-you're-gonna-soil-your-shorts kind of lion.

He's crouched down. He's looking at you. He roars. It's *loud*. You jump. You're afraid. Who wouldn't be?

The best lion trainers in the world would shake in their boots because this guy is not their friend, and they know exactly the devastation a beast like this can cause.

And who are you? What do you have to defend yourself? Strength? A gun? Fast feet? Nope. You're not going to win. Not with this cat.

You're supposed to be afraid. Look at the picture the disciple Peter drew.

BE ALERT AND OF SOBER MIND. YOUR ENEMY THE DEVIL PROWLS AROUND LIKE A ROARING LION LOOKING FOR SOMEONE TO DEVOUR. (1 PETER 5:8)

We often come up with our own imagery and metaphor to help us understand Scripture, but this imagery is from God. That's why it's worth our contemplation.

Do you get the idea that Satan and the sin we're tempted with is kid's stuff? Not in God's eyes. We better not take it lightly, either. Let's recognize the destruction Satan really wants to stir up as we try to peacefully mind our own business.

Never be deceived by what this lion may have up his paw. It is NEVER—no way, no how—in your best interest. He doesn't intend to scratch you, disappoint you, or leave you requiring a mere tetanus shot. He means to destroy, shred, and tear to pieces every ounce of well-being and joy in your soul.

Don't ever fight this beast on your own. Don't try talking back to it. You can't win it over. Don't give it a command and expect it to obey. Can you imagine a lion sitting and purring just because you told him to?

When we say the Lord is mighty in battle, just what kind of battle do you think we're talking about?

Lion hunting. That's what we're talking about.

God is mighty. So you're safe.

HE WILL COVER YOU WITH HIS FEATHERS, AND UNDER HIS WINGS YOU WILL FIND REFUGE; HIS FAITHFULNESS WILL BE YOUR SHIELD AND RAMPART. (PSALM 91:4)

When thoughts come to your mind, and you're tempted to lie, cheat, act immorally, or whatever your weakness may be, look around. You're not alone. Look close enough and you'll see a lion somewhere. But don't freak out. Now you know what to do, right?

SO HUMBLE YOURSELVES BEFORE GOD. RESIST THE DEVIL, AND HE WILL FLEE FROM YOU. (JAMES 4:7 NLT)

From humility comes power. What an unlikely place to acquire power. The world would never think up that idea. Humbly submitting yourself to God means a total trust in God's strength and not your own. (Might want to read that last sentence one more time, because way too many battle-weary folk seem to miss it.)

God goes before you with a shield (or maybe sometimes a whip and a chair). And just when Satan assumes you've fallen prey, this lion has no choice but to turn tail and run. He ain't messin' with Jesus. Even *he* knows how futile *that* would be. Let Jesus fight your battle for you. Ask him to. You won't need to ask twice.

Go back to I Peter 5:8. What's the first thing it says? *Be alert.* This means you need to keep your wits about you. Don't underestimate just where a lion might go or how hungry he might be.

Also, this verse tells you to keep out of the jungle where lions are looking for lunch. Where's the jungle? That's an important question to answer if you're going to be able to avoid it. Is it the bar, the fridge, the Internet, the bookstore, the bedroom, or anyplace you can gossip, steal something, or be lazy?

Jungles aren't always well marked, so don't let your guard down.

CHAPTER 21

SOMETIMES I FEEL UNSURE

His name was John.

He was a little different—but aren't we all, really?

No, he was more than a little different.

He lived alone.

(In the desert of all places.)

He wore a leather belt.

(That's kind of cool.)

But it was to hold up his camel kilt.

(Okay, maybe not so cool.)

He ate grasshoppers.

(A good source of protein.)

He didn't drink.

(Though some probably thought he did.)

He took on everybody.

Did I mention he was called demon-possessed more than once?

He was out in the desert yelling, "Hey, you want a piece of me?" Forgive me, that's so not what he said—I just wanted to be sure I had your attention. (You can read about what he really said in the book of John.) But he was out in the desert, and he was ready for any confrontation that came his way. He called the religious leaders a brood of snakes and announced they were basically on their way to hell. That probably went over well, don't you think?

People, this was not a man who waffled.

He sat on no fence.

He was on fire.

And he was single-minded.

People came from all over to hear him and be baptized by him. He preached one message—Jesus is coming, so get your heart ready.

He was hard to ignore. He even caught the attention of King Herod Antipas, the ruler of Galilee. Now this is where it all starts to get interesting—as if a guy like this isn't colorful enough.

He had the guts, and I mean *guts*, to tell Herod to stop messing around with his sister-in-law. Herod stole his half-brother's wife and dumped his own. The Bible describes Herod Antipas as somebody who really piled on the sins. In fact, John let Herod have it on all the areas of his life that were misguided. Herod was one cruel son of a gun, so—believe me— there were a few things to talk about. Which is why you'd assume John would leave him alone.

If we're honest with ourselves, I bet most of us would.

Why badger Herod about his lifestyle? He's the king. Kings do what they want. Kings mess around. Kings cut people's heads off if the soup has too much salt. John was pretty bold for a guy in a camel skirt.

But what really made Herod nervous was John's influence with the people. They didn't just stroll out to the desert to check him out. They traveled from all over to "see and hear" him. He was a destination. John stirred people up, and his message changed people's lives.

Herod could just see that coming to no good end. He had visions of being overthrown by a country full of religious freaks.

So he put John in prison. Even so, there's reason to believe that Herod, at some level, really liked John. His message must've been a hard pill to swallow, but there was something about the goodness and heart of John that Herod came to admire. It leads you to believe that John balanced his message with both truth and grace.

In fact while John was in prison, Herod didn't forget him.

HEROD KNEW THAT JOHN WAS A FAIR AND HOLY MAN, SO HE PROTECTED HIM. WHEN HE LISTENED TO JOHN, HE WOULD BECOME VERY DISTURBED, AND YET HE LIKED TO LISTEN TO HIM. (MARK 6:20 GOD'S WORD)

(Causing a disturbance is not foreign to the brave of heart.)

Then came Herod's birthday party—a crazy, drunken hullabaloo with dancing girls and lots of food. John may have even heard the music.

He may have heard the very tune that accompanied the beautiful, graceful dancer named Salome who made Herod's birthday party something we still talk about today.

It was probably late into the evening, and Herod may have been overserved, but he was so thrilled with the performance that he offered Salome anything she wanted—up to half the kingdom. Wow.

Salome was Herod's niece—daughter of the woman he stole from his brother. Her mother's name was Herodias, and you can just imagine how she felt about John—a man who wouldn't let up about the error of her marriage to such a powerful man.

So, she dictated the wish of her daughter, Salome: John's head on a platter. His head is one thing—but on a platter? She didn't want to just hear about it, she wanted to see his head on a platter with her own eyes. Class act, wasn't she?

But what a nice and tidy solution to a man who made himself a nuisance to them. In fact, it might've even pleased Herod.

But Herod was sad.

The impact John had on the lives of those he touched needs to be noted. A life well lived is not quickly forgotten.

SURELY THE RIGHTEOUS...WILL BE REMEMBERED FOREVER. (PSALM 112:6)

Now Herod had made this promise in front of a palace full of people, so it was a matter of "integrity" to keep his word. It appears the beheading happened in short order.

But not before John asked a question.

He made so many declarations out in that desert wilderness, but in the depths of his dark, dank prison cell he had a question. Just one.

He asked his friends, the disciples, to ask Jesus if he was who he said he was...or, "should we look for somebody else?"

Friends, this man of steel was broken. He was unsure. He was not so certain he sold out for the right man. This question of his is one of the most heart-stopping in all of the New Testament.

John wondered.

John had never wondered, never wavered, never wimped out.

But he was broken, and it's interesting where the mind can go in desperate situations, isn't it?

How many times do we find ourselves looking for someone else?

Now, of course, we need to know how this story ends. We need to know because when we're broken, we need to know if Jesus is who he says he is.

Jesus answered John with proof that doesn't have any loopholes in it. He sent his disciples back to tell John how lives were changing in unmistakable, inarguable ways.

The blind were seeing.

The lame were walking.

The sick were made well.

The dead were being raised to life.

The deaf could hear.

People were hearing the good news.

And then Jesus added, "How happy is he who has no doubts about me!"

He added that because a secure heart is a heart at rest. And that's what Jesus wanted for John. And that's what he wants for us, too.

He had no trouble with John's question. He surely has no trouble with yours, either. If he hears from you, I promise you'll hear from him. Expect him to answer you in an assuring, no-loophole kind of way.

I SOUGHT THE LORD AND HE ANSWERED ME; HE DELIVERED ME FROM ALL MY FEARS. (PSALM 34:4)

Jesus did allow John to die for his faith. It seems a harsh close to a life lived with so much passion—kind of like a fairy tale without a happy ending. Evil woman beheads the hero. But from an eternal perspective, John really does live happily ever after.

He lived for something he was willing to die for and could say with King David who went before him—

SURELY I HAVE A DELIGHTFUL INHERITANCE. (PSALM 16:6)

Jesus loved him before he was born.

HE [JOHN] WILL BE GREAT IN THE SIGHT OF THE LORD. (LUKE 1:15)

And he missed him after he died.

JOHN WAS A LAMP THAT BURNED AND GAVE LIGHT. (JOHN 5:35)

Jesus was proud of his friend and he answered John at the most unsure moment of his life with certainty we can all trust.

I bet there was a big feast in heaven when those two finally laid eyes on each other again.

(Think they ate grasshoppers?)

CHAPTER 22

SOMETIMES I FEEL ANONYMOUS

The grocery store can be a rather humbling experience. If you want a little shaved turkey, you pull a number off a dispenser on the counter. Then you stand there. You're nameless and faceless. You'd be totally ignored for who knows how long without that little paper tab with the number 36 to identify your needs. That number secures your right to buy a piece of turkey.

If you're like most, you probably use *another* number to now pay for your turkey. It doesn't really matter who you are as long as the numbers on that little plastic card are legit.

Employed? I bet you have an employee number.

Have a birth certificate? You have a social security number.

Save a little money? You have a bank account number.

Those numbers keep track of you.

In some instances they may even define you.

But they can't possibly let anyone know who you are or what you're all about.

They don't tell if you had a good day at school, if you like your job, or if your boyfriend just broke up with you. That social security number doesn't tell anyone how you felt when your dad left.

Here's a reassuring thought:

GOD DOESN'T COUNT US. HE CALLS US BY NAME. (ROMANS 9:28 MSG)

Among the masses, most of us are nameless and faceless. With our Heavenly Friend, each of us is a multidimensional human being with lots of stories, experiences, emotions, troubles, talents, and disappointments. And each of us has a name.

A name he knew way before even your parents thought it up.

He keeps it close at hand.

LOOK, I HAVE CARVED YOUR NAME IN MY HAND. I THINK ABOUT YOU ALL THE TIME. (ISAIAH 49:16 ETR)

What amazes you more? That God knows you by name, or that he thinks about you all the time? There's a picture of genuine love being drawn here. Don't be like so many who never see how close their relationships with God can be.

You are never *hey you, what's-her-name* or number 3,367,899 of the human race. Your Heavenly Father will never call you by your brother's name by mistake, either. Nope. He knows you intimately and personally and, okay, I'll say it again—by name. Even if you haven't taken the time to get to know *him* that well, he knows you.

I AM THE GOD OF ISRAEL AND I AM CALLING YOU BY NAME! ISAIAH 45:3 (ERV)

This name-calling is a two-way street with God.

He calls our name.

And we call on his.

It's understandable if you're feeling a little bit special about now.

CHAPTER 23

SOMETIMES I FEEL SELF-IMPORTANT

Ever been around somebody who thought he was a little better than everybody else? We all have. It's not hard to come up with a joker or two meeting that criterion. And truth be told, odds are pretty good our name appears on that list from time to time.

Go ahead and add the disciples to that list, too. Yup. The disciples. The original dozen who ate, drank, fished, and laughed with Jesus.

Here's what happened. All 12 of them were on a dirty road heading for Capernaum. (See Mark 9:33-35.) I may be going out on a limb here, but most likely they were a little tired, a little hungry, and therefore, a little crabby. We don't know all that for sure, but clearly they started acting like a bunch of five-year-olds.

They started arguing about who was better than whom.

We can only imagine they were not in good humor upon arriving at their destination. I bet Jesus would've loved to have given all 12 of them a time-out in the market square. But rather than humiliate them in public, Jesus lovingly waited for just the right time to address the issue.

WHEN HE WAS SAFE AT HOME, HE ASKED THEM, "WHAT WERE YOU DISCUSSING ON THE ROAD?" (MARK 9:33 MSG)

Discussing? Jesus knew full well what they were discussing. So, what did they do? Right. They didn't answer him. (Don't look surprised. We've all pulled that one before.)

THE SILENCE WAS DEAFENING—THEY HAD BEEN ARGUING WITH ONE ANOTHER OVER WHO AMONG THEM WAS GREATEST. (MARK 9:34 MSG)

So Jesus called them together. I can just imagine how he handled it:

"You want to be in first place? Look, you could have just asked because I'm glad to tell you."

We're not told, but I can only guess that once again the silence was deafening. They were about to be given a secret from the keeper of all secrets, and not a one of them was about to miss this gem.

And the answer is....be last. Be a servant of all.

They may have asked to have that one repeated.

The message isn't that astounding if you've gotten to know this Jesus of ours at all. He's looking for hearts ready to see the needs of others and serve those needs. He's looking for hearts that don't hold themselves in higher esteem than those around them.

That doesn't mean fame, fortune, responsibility, and power may not come your way. In fact, that may be quite likely. But you are to examine your heart and see if your motivation is right with God. It's not about your position; it's about your attitude.

Later on Jesus was with these same 12 friends he loved so much. He confided in them the details of his future—the whips, the beatings, the cross. It couldn't have been an easy conversation.

On the heels of this revelation, James and John (they're brothers) pulled Jesus aside and spoke to him. "Teacher," they said, "we want you to do us a favor" (Mark 10:35 NLT).

Honestly, they called it a favor.

So what might you guess they're after?

Loaves of bread because Jesus seems to so often have a few to spare?

An extra tunic because they left theirs at Martha's house?

A pair of sandals because a strap broke?

Not exactly.

They asked for a couple of thrones. Not thrones just anywhere, but thrones that would be placed on either side of Jesus when they all got to heaven.

What would you give to see the look on Jesus' face?

We don't have that Kodak moment, but we do know what he said. (See Mark 10:35-45.)

"What are ya, nuts?"

No, no, no. Just kidding. He's not like us.

Instead he replied, "You don't know what you're asking for."

He sounds so patient with these lugheads, doesn't he? That's awesome news for us because you know as well as I do that from time to time we, too, are lugheads who expect thrones to sit on.

Jesus went on to explain that it really isn't up to him. The Father makes those calls.

Who will be on those thrones? God only knows, but you can be sure it'll be somebody who really understood the idea of what it means to serve.

So hurry up and get to the back of the line, ya lughead.

CHAPTER 24
SOMETIMES I FEEL PROUD

Power and prestige can really mess with a person. We don't have to look too far to find examples. Give somebody a movie deal, a fancy title, or a recording contract, and life can go haywire before you hire a publicist, chauffeur, or style consultant.

In fact, while character can be tested in many ways, the book of Proverbs tells us success is definitely a barometer of what we're made of.

We can also look to the Old Testament and find kings who were appointed to rule over God's people, who had some trouble keeping their crowns on straight. Centuries come and go but, interestingly, people stay pretty much the same.

Let's spend some time with one of the kings who actually got it right—and he was one of the youngest. King Hezekiah. He was just a young man really—25 years old—when he took over his father's throne. His father, King Ahaz, left him quite a mess. We would put Ahaz in the category of those kings who didn't get it right. He turned his back on God, and the place went downhill fast.

Put yourself in Hezekiah's sandals. You're 25 and, basically, your wish is everyone's command. What would you do? Be honest. Order up some fast chariots? Cool tunics? Exotic food? A regal game of soccer? (Hey, I'm sure they played some version of it.) A party for all the who's who of Judah? A refreshing mud bath? All understandable, for this royalty business is heady stuff.

During Hezekiah's first month in power, he chose to fix up the temple. (That also may have been on your list. I have no way of knowing.)

The temple was in a shambles, which reflected the condition of the people's hearts. But our young friend, the king, wouldn't tolerate the people of God acting like a bunch of pagans. So, in short order, he got the repairs accomplished and sent messengers all over the land proclaiming the good news. They didn't have newspapers, mail, or news conferences. They were simply men on horses exhorting the people to turn their hearts around...and they had a little help.

AND GOD UNITED ALL THE PEOPLE OF JUDAH IN OBEYING KING HEZEKIAH AND HIS OFFICERS, BECAUSE THEIR COMMAND HAD COME FROM THE LORD. (2 CHRONICLES 30:12 NCV)

This is noteworthy because it means it's not all up to us. If we follow and trust in the Lord, he makes our efforts fruitful.

So the people came. They came in great numbers to Jerusalem to celebrate the Passover at the new temple. You think you know how to party? Ever do it for a week and think it was so much fun you extended it for seven more days? That's what happened in Jerusalem. There was food, music, worship, fellowship, and encouragement. Good times. Good times. Nothing like that had happened in years, and people were pumped up.

See what happens when just one young person follows God's heart?

And we're just getting started.

Hezekiah didn't do anything you couldn't do, by the way. Oh, he had a secret, but it's nothing beyond you:

HE SOUGHT HIS GOD AND WORKED WHOLEHEARTEDLY. AND SO HE PROSPERED. (2 CHRONICLES 31:21)

Wholeheartedly. Don't you love that word? Don't you hate halfhearted attempts at anything? Isn't it halfhearted attitudes that make this world an irritating place?

You also gotta love the word *prospered.*

And let me tell you how Hezekiah prospered at the gracious hand of his Heavenly Father. Barns, barns, and more barns full of stuff everybody would love to have—food, wine, silver, gold, animals, spices, precious stones, you name it.

Unfortunately, prosperity can be a two-edged sword. The minute you've got a little something for yourself, isn't it just like some knucklehead to come along and want to take it from you? Enter Sennacherib, the King of Assyria. He saw all the good stuff over there in the land of Judah and wanted it. So he made plans for war.

The people of Judah didn't take kindly to that. Well, actually, they freaked out. But King Hezekiah really earned his crown that day. He calmed everybody down and rallied the troops with a little dose of truth and encouragement.

He said, "Look, these people are relying on their own strength to win this battle, but the Lord our God is with us." Impressive young man, isn't he?

Way to keep one's head on one's shoulders.

King Sennacherib mocked the whole "God thing," made a fool of himself and his entire army, and was then annihilated by the Lord's angel. (Yeah, that's right. One angel.) So they all went home—with their tails between their legs, we could quite accurately add. Had Hezekiah been proud and fought in his own strength, this story would have had a much different ending.

Everybody almost lived happily ever after. It seems as though the story should end here, but it doesn't. It's not quite the perfect fairy tale, so don't miss the next chapter.

CHAPTER 25

SOMETIMES I FEEL STUBBORN

So did Hezekiah.

All his success ended up doing a number on King Hezekiah's heart. Can you guess what got the best of him? I know you said *pride*.

But beyond pride, Hezekiah dug his heels in the ground and got stubborn about the path he was going down. He didn't easily turn around. You know how we can be about our paths, don't you? We can get pretty certain and convinced about our choices and ideas. But as dogged as we may be, can you imagine how God might stick to his guns until he wins? Especially when it involves our hearts. God doesn't surrender you without a fierce fight. But what good dad would?

Hezekiah's wake-up call consisted of an illness that brought him to the brink of death. The Lord was tapping him on the shoulder, and Hezekiah did indeed look to the Lord for help and healing. God, full of graciousness, took away Hezekiah's suffering in a way that's characterized as miraculous. We don't really have the details, but we know it was extraordinary. (See 2 Chronicles 32:24-33.)

Do you know that wasn't enough to knock Hezekiah off his high horse? He was *still proud*. All his success and good health didn't produce a thankful heart in him. If you're ready to smack him upside his head about now, imagine how God felt.

When miracles and goodness don't produce God's intended results, sometimes God changes tactics. The Lord wasn't going to walk away from Hezekiah, but Hezekiah wasn't about to change his ways. So it gets a little ugly. I'm quite sure there's a lesson in there for us, and I don't think I have to spell it out.

(Okay, I won't spell it out, but I'll put it right here, really small in parentheses in case anybody is scratching her head. Here's what we better learn: Listen to God the first time. On the road trip of life—don't make your Dad stop the car.)

Again, we don't know the details, but the Bible says Hezekiah felt God's wrath. I'm sure the Lord can make that felt quite effectively. And effective it was, because it was that trial that brought Hezekiah to his knees.

It was a trial so severe it finally brought him to repentance... and you know the rest of the story. Repentance makes our God in heaven dance a jig and turn cartwheels. So, in the end, Hezekiah did get it right. He stumbled, but he didn't fall.

Now we come to one of the most curious events in Hezekiah's story. All the success in the land of Judah caught the attention of many nations. Babylon actually sent an envoy to ask basically one question: "What gives?" They wanted to know what was behind all the good fortune in this land.

That in and of itself isn't so curious. We should expect people to be curious about the source of blessing in our lives, shouldn't we?

But I guarantee that what God did next will stop you in your tracks.

God left Hezekiah.

Scripture tells us why.

God left Hezekiah to test him—in order to hear his honest heartfelt answer to this curious Babylonian.

Of course God knew it, but he wanted to hear from Hezekiah's own lips what was going on in his heart. Isn't that touching? God hears the praise of angels and saints on a continual basis. Jesus said he could make the stones cry out and praise him if he wanted.

But God wanted to hear that, in Hezekiah's heart of hearts, he loved and honored the Lord.

Your words are powerful.

God listens to them.

Make his day. Tell him you love him. Tell somebody else you love him. Then feel him smile at you. He won't be able to help himself.

CHAPTER 26

SOMETIMES I FEEL RESTLESS

If you or I were calling the shots, we wouldn't dream of asking Jesus to spend his first night on earth in a cow's feeding trough. Nor would we put him out on the dusty roads of Galilee without an address or a pillow for his head.

These circumstances don't befit a king.

But the truth is that you and I aren't much better off. We're homeless, too. Even though at this very moment you may be reading this book from the comfort of an overstuffed couch, feeling anything but homeless.

You are not home.

You are on your way home.

But you are not home.

That's why this earthly place we try to make home doesn't always feel so comfy cozy.

We really weren't created to live here forever.

Not like this, we weren't.

There's something in that last paragraph that rings true with you, isn't there? There are moments of *something just is not right* that we all experience because something in this world really is not right.

We weren't created to live in a fallen world, and we weren't created to die. Something in all of us tells us there HAS TO BE MORE THAN THIS.

And we're right. Our DNA and the Bible tell us so.

HE HAS ALSO SET ETERNITY IN THE HUMAN HEART; YET NO ONE CAN FATHOM WHAT GOD HAS DONE FROM BEGINNING TO END. (ECCLESIASTES 3:11)

So there it is. We know there's something more than this, but we can't see the big picture. We aren't given the entire plan, but we're given just enough of it so we can look forward to what's ahead of us. Just like so many have done before us.

How did they do it?

THEY SAW IT WAY OFF IN THE DISTANCE, WAVED THEIR GREETING, AND ACCEPTED THE FACT THAT THEY WERE TRANSIENTS IN THIS WORLD. PEOPLE WHO LIVE THIS WAY MAKE IT PLAIN THAT THEY ARE LOOKING FOR THEIR TRUE HOME. (HEBREWS 11:13-14 MSG)

We're pilgrims, but we're not wanderers. Wanderers don't know where they're going, or why they're on the path.

We know full well what our life here is all about. On our way home we're taking as many with us as possible. We're pointing the way with our lives.

Just because we're homeless doesn't mean we're not joyful. Having purpose and being protected, loved, and guided does not a downtrodden person make.

Easy? Not always. Not by a long shot.

But temporary. Only temporary.

So we keep on truckin'.

INSTEAD, THEY WERE LONGING FOR A BETTER COUNTRY—A HEAVENLY ONE. THEREFORE GOD IS NOT ASHAMED TO BE CALLED THEIR GOD, FOR HE HAS PREPARED A CITY FOR THEM. (HEBREWS 11:16)

When you arrive there'll be no mistaking whether or not you were expected. Oh no...all the stops will be pulled out to celebrate your homecoming. Don't think you'll be greeted by some heavenly maid or butler who'll escort you to the royal salon for a robe fitting and makeover before entering the throne room.

No, no, no. Your Heavenly Father will be waiting. His arms will be open, his smile will be wide, his eyes will be sparkling, and you'll know. Oh, my friend, will you ever know. This is what it was all about. This is why you steadfastly stuck it out.

You'll feel your Father's love, and then you'll hear him brag about you. For a minute you might look around to see who he's talking about, but he'll be looking right at you, and these words will never sound so sweet:

"WELL DONE, GOOD AND FAITHFUL SERVANT! YOU HAVE BEEN FAITHFUL WITH A FEW THINGS; I WILL PUT YOU IN CHARGE OF MANY THINGS. COME AND SHARE YOUR MASTER'S HAPPINESS!" (MATTHEW 25:21)

I bet I know what you're thinking right now: *I can imagine him saying that about a few people I know, but not me. I really haven't done much for him at all.*

When you belong to God, you're perfect in his eyes. Jesus died to see you as such. God doesn't remember your imperfections because, let's see, where have those gone? Yes, they would be at the bottom of the ocean. A place where nobody finds them or even goes looking—including God. In absence of all your sin your Father only sees perfection, so that's why he has such glowing words for you.

Once that's understood you can boldly say:

I HAVE FOUGHT THE GOOD FIGHT, I HAVE FINISHED THE RACE, AND I HAVE KEPT THE FAITH. (2 TIMOTHY 4:7)

Some say life is short. But that depends on your perspective, doesn't it?

CHAPTER 27

SOMETIMES I FEEL UNDESERVING

Let's consider, for a moment, the transition from this world to the next.

It's sure to be quite a grand moment, meeting this Jesus of ours face-to-face for the first time. He's going to have a conversation with each and every one of us. It seems like that would take too long, but God's got eternity and no better place to go...so make yourself comfortable.

How might it go?

"Now, you lived in a pretty big house, didn't you?"

"No, not really. I mean, it was just a three-bedroom Cape Cod."

"Oh. Well, you belonged to a country club, though, right?"

"I never played golf."

"Never golfed, huh?"

"No, just a little neighborhood kickball."

"No sports scholarship?"

"No."

"Don't worry. Uh...let's see...Oh! How about awards? An Oscar?"

"No."

"Grammy?"

"Uh uh."

"Nobel Peace Prize?"

"Nope. To my knowledge they never considered me."

"Yeah, that was a long shot. How about Most Likely to Succeed?"

"Not that, either."

"Spelling bee?"

"Actually, yes. It would've been in the fourth grade."

If you're getting the idea that God won't care much about our earthly accomplishments at the end of the line, you're right. In fact, in light of eternity, the things we fret about and chase after almost seem a little silly. But don't be confused. Our abilities and accomplishments are important (they're gifts from God, so don't take them lightly), but they aren't the *most* important.

Nope. It'll come down to one thing—your heart. Did you let God have it?

If you believe God will consider that you were decent most of the time, and honest most of the time, and reasonably thoughtful most of the time, and thereby open wide heaven's door for you—you're wrong. And if you're on the other side, thinking God will never let you in because of all the terrible things you've done—you're wrong.

Here's a great story to help us understand why passing through the pearly gates has nothing to do with what we do. It's about what he did.

The man was nameless. By "happenstance" he was sentenced to die on the same day, at the same time, in the same place, in the same way as Jesus.

He was being crucified and, by his own admission, it was a death he deserved. His crimes probably went beyond thievery—we don't have his rap sheet but you can fill in the blanks.

Hanging on the cross with nails in his hands and feet made breathing one of his most difficult tasks. This fact puts his behavior in perspective—he used some of those precious breaths to make fun of Jesus.

EVEN THE MEN WHO WERE CRUCIFIED WITH JESUS RIDICULED HIM. (MARK 15:32 NLT)

He felt superior enough to poke a little fun at this man beside him who was supposed to save the world and wouldn't even save himself.

Maybe he hung a little taller because he wasn't wearing that humiliating crown of thorns.

As the horror of this Friday afternoon unfolded, something about the King of the Jews became clear and melted this hardened criminal's heart. Maybe it was hearing Jesus forgive the soldiers who wielded the hammers and taunted him while he died. Maybe hearing Jesus provide for his mother touched the criminal's heart.

WHEN JESUS SAW HIS MOTHER THERE, AND THE DISCIPLE WHOM HE LOVED STANDING NEARBY, HE SAID TO HER, "WOMAN, HERE IS YOUR SON," AND TO THE DISCIPLE, "HERE IS YOUR MOTHER." FROM THAT TIME ON, THIS DISCIPLE TOOK HER INTO HIS HOME. (JOHN 19: 26-27)

Or maybe he caught a look in Jesus' eye that made this criminal actually feel loved. Even him.

At some instant he realized exactly what he was witnessing. All his guilt was being paid for.

At some moment he gave his heart to Jesus.

This is beautiful. The unnamed thief asked Jesus to remember him when Jesus got to heaven. The response he heard would've made him kick up his heels and clap his hands if only he were able: "As sure as my name is Jesus, I'll see you there later today."

(I paraphrased a little bit, but you can read it in Luke 23.)

Now, here's the grand point of the story: Did this guy live a life that earned him a spot at the family table in heaven? Not exactly. But he had assurance from the very lips of Jesus that he was heaven-bound. Undeserving? Yeah. But that's grace for you. This thief did nothing. Jesus did it all. Our partner in crime simply opened his heart.

So, ask yourself, my friend.

Who has your heart?

APPENDIX

SOMETIMES I FEEL LIKE I HAVE MAIL

Following is a letter to you.

God wrote it.

And it's addressed to you.

The contents come directly from God's Word—all Bible verses—just rearranged a little.

Dear _____, (that's a little spot for your name)

Know that when you speak, your voice is heard. In fact, I bend down to listen to you. So come to me as long as you live.

Tell me your troubles. When you're overwhelmed, I know the way you should turn.

I'll direct every step you take. Even if you stumble along the way, you won't fall because I'll be holding your hand. I delight in every detail of your life—right down to the number of hairs on your head.

I'll go before you to prepare the way, and I'll follow behind you to protect you. My hand is always on you.

If you ever feel afraid, understand that's not me. I don't give you a spirit of fear but rather one of power and love. It is my power that strengthens you. So don't give up when troubles come—instead, be patient.

I will fight for you. Just stay calm. You are hidden in the shadow of my wings.

Every day I pick up your burdens so you don't have to carry them. I do that because I love you so dearly—in fact my love knows no bounds.

You are precious to me; I will guard you as the apple of my eye. And know that the One who watches over you never sleeps. It is always better to find your refuge in me than to trust in people.

I enjoy doing good things for you. With all of who I am I want to make you grow like a well-watered garden. I will send showers—showers of blessings just when you need them.

I have so many plans for you—you can't even list them. These are plans to prosper you, not harm you. Plans that give you a future and a hope.

You can trust me with all of your heart. Fix your thoughts on me, and I will keep you in perfect peace.

I'll make your face radiant and fill your heart with joy.

You might even find yourself singing.

I've made this day, so enjoy it.

Love,

Your Dad

BIBLE VERSES IN ORDER OF APPEARANCE

I love the Lord because he hears my voice and my prayer for mercy. Because he bends down to listen, I will pray as long as I have breath! (Psalm 116:1-2 NLT)

I pour out my complaints before him and tell him all my troubles. When I am overwhelmed, you alone know the way I should turn. (Psalm 142:2-3 NLT)

The Lord directs the steps of the godly. He delights in every detail of their lives. Though they stumble, they will never fall, for the Lord holds them by the hand. (Psalm 37:23-24 NLT)

And the very hairs on your head are all numbered. (Mathew 10:30 NLT)

You go before me and follow me. You place your hand of blessing on my head. (Psalm 139:5 NLT)

For God has not given us a spirit of fear and timidity, but of power, love, and self-discipline. (2 Timothy 1:7 NLT)

God will strengthen you with his own great power so that you will not give up when troubles come, but you will be patient. (Colossians 1:11 NCV)

"Don't be afraid. Just stand still and watch the Lord rescue you today. The Egyptians you see today will never be seen again. The Lord himself will fight for you. Just stay calm." (Exodus 14: 13-14 NLT)

Hide me in the shadow of your wings. (Psalm 17:8 NLT)

Praise be to the Lord, to God our Savior, who daily bears our burdens. (Psalm 68:19)

Be imitators of God, therefore, as dearly loved children. (Ephesians 5:1 NIV)

The Lord says, "...my love will know no bounds, for my anger will be gone forever." (Hosea 14:4 NLT)

Others were given in exchange for you. I traded their lives for yours because you are precious to me. You are honored, and I love you. (Isaiah 43:4 NLT)

Keep me as the apple of your eye... (Psalm 17:8 NIV)

He who guards you never sleeps. (Psalm 121:3 NCV)

It is better to take refuge in the LORD than to trust in people. (Psalm 118:8 NLT)

I will rejoice in doing them good and will assuredly plant them in this land with all my heart and soul. (Jeremiah 32:41)

And in the proper season I will send the showers they need. There will be showers of blessing. (Ezekiel 34:26 NLT)

Your plans for us are too numerous to list. (Psalm 40:5 NLT)

"For I know the plans I have for you," says the LORD. "They are plans for good and not for disaster, to give you a future and a hope." (Jeremiah 29:11 NLT)

You will keep in perfect peace all who trust in you, all whose thoughts are fixed on you! (Isaiah 26:3 NLT)

Those who look to him for help will be radiant with joy; no shadow of shame will darken their faces. (Psalm 34:5 NLT)

The LORD is my strength and shield. I trust him with all my heart. He helps me, and my heart is filled with joy. I burst out in songs of thanksgiving. (Psalm 28:7 NLT)

This is the day the LORD has made. We will rejoice and be glad in it. (Psalm 118:24 NLT)